Mel Gibson

Mel Gibson

PETER CARRICK

ROBERT HALE · LONDON

Photoset in North Wales by
Derek Doyle & Associates, Mold, Flintshire
Printed in Great Britain by
St Edmundsbury Press Limited, Bury St Edmunds
and bound by
WBC Book Manufacturers Limited, Bridgend

Contents

For Brenda, Sarah and Deborah
. . . for making everything worth while

Acknowledgements

Sources in Australia, the United States and the United Kingdom have been of considerable help to me in compiling this biography of Mel Gibson. My sincere thanks and appreciation for their time and interest are extended to them all.

Australia
Barbara Amer, Asquith Boys High School, Australian Film Commission, Belvoir Theatre, Broken Hill City Library (Kathy Bennett, Outback Archives), Audrey Bourke, Macquarie Tourist Office, National Institute of Dramatic Art, St Leo's College, Sydney, Sydney City Library.

United States
Laurens Central School, New York State (Nancy Johnson, Media Specialist).

United Kingdom
Neil Ajmal, Australian High Commission (London), Moira Barron, *Big Issue in Scotland*, Rita Boyce, British Film Institute, Joan Buckle, John Cohen, Edna Ellis, Ted Ellis, Brian Gayler, Albert Gearing, Hertfordshire Library Service (Baldock and Letchworth Garden City branches), Ron Millett, Don Shiach, John Walter Skinner, United States Information Service.

Some sources wished to remain anonymous and although they are not acknowledged here, I am grateful to them for their time, interest and contributions. Other important sources of information were *Mel Gibson* (Comet) by David Ragan; *Reluctant Star*

(Fontana) by James Oram; *Mel, the Inside Story* (Blake) by Wensley Clarkson; and *Lethal Hero* (Oliver Books) by Roland Perry.

I would like to extend my particular thanks and gratitude to Frances-M Blake, who allowed me access to her extensive and detailed records, documentation and information on Mel Gibson, and for her continuing interest, encouragement and help during the researching and writing of this book.

Please note that the text shows American dollars ($), unless otherwise stated.

Illustrations

Between pages 152 and 153

Illustration Credits

Ted Ellis: 1, 2. British Film Institute: 3–22.

Prologue: The Ten-Million-Dollar Man

Being a movie actor can be an uncertain, traumatic business. Struggling early days carry no guarantee of ultimate success and the most illustrious reputations can be shattered by a couple of indifferent pictures. But the American-born young man who had already conquered his adopted Australia and whose talent and charisma had some time before created a sensation in Hollywood felt no such feelings of insecurity in 1990.

For much of the past nine years Mel Gibson had been one of the hottest properties in worldwide cinema. His international breakthrough came with his sensitive performance in the 1981 Australian-made movie *Gallipoli*, for which he received just $A35,000, a modest enough sum even then.

Hollywood spotted his potential and decided it was time to take over, making him a star with the oldest trick in the movie-making book. They simply took his earlier triumph in *Mad Max*, released a year before *Gallipoli* came out and which would go on to become the most successful Australian picture ever made, and recreated his role of Max Rockatansky. The sequel shamelessly exploited the kind of impressive all-action sequences that had captured so much attention in the original Gothic-horror 'Max' movie. Seldom shy of putting money where its hunches are, Hollywood assigned a healthy budget to *Mad Max 2* (*The Road Warrior* in the United States) and showed some generosity of spirit in paying Gibson $100,000 to continue the role he had already made his own. In the United States alone the picture grossed $24 million and made the charts in most critics' top ten movies of 1982.

Mel Gibson would go on to make headlines both on and off

11

the silver screen in the following years. His partiality for routinely stepping into bars, some of doubtful reputation, was set alongside the instant and almost hypnotic appeal he held for many women. Both claimed as many column inches in fan magazines and the tabloid press as did his soaring reputation as a movie star.

His versatility matched his astonishing mass appeal, stretching from his role as Fletcher Christian in a remake of *Mutiny on the Bounty* to his unexpected triumph in the Franco Zeffirelli version of Shakespeare's *Hamlet*. But the picture which brought him headline-making fame and made him one of the most bankable of all Hollywood stars was released in 1987. Hollywood again returned to a winning formula, casting him with Danny Glover, Gary Busey and Mitchell Ryan in the all-action stunt movie, *Lethal Weapon*. The picture captured the public mood of the moment for big-screen action movies. Gibson played Martin Riggs, highly trained in the precision skills of CIA covert operations and a former member of a crack Special Forces unit during the Vietnam war, but himself now registered as a 'lethal weapon' within the Los Angeles Police Department.

Lethal Weapon grossed $65 million in the United States alone, but owed almost as much of its success to the dynamic interplay between Gibson and Glover as it did to its high-speed violence and all-action plot. As the picture-makers pointed out: 'Martin Riggs is the only LA cop registered as a "Lethal Weapon" . . . Glover carries a weapon, Gibson is one.' Both are single operators who hate to work with partners. They have nothing in common.

Gibson as Riggs is a killing machine befitting his battle background and his present uncompromising lifestyle. He is many years younger than Glover, who plays Roger Murtaugh, a Vietnam veteran, devoted family man and facing fifty with some trepidation. He is a homicide detective with a solid reputation and an unblemished department record. But as a studio executive explained: 'Cops don't get to choose their partners. That's the job of the department. And Riggs and Murtaugh are forced to form an uneasy alliance as they begin to unravel the mystery of an apparent suicide that turns out to be murder . . . and much more.'

Warner Brothers were delighted with the success of *Lethal Weapon*. It turned in more money than they had expected and

brought big attention-grabbing headlines. Gibson was not altogether happy with the level of violence in the picture, but quickly put it behind him when accepting a fee of $1.5 million to head
the cast of *Tequila Sunrise* alongside Michelle Pfeiffer and Kurt
Russell. But this, disappointingly, was another 'buddy-buddy'
movie rather dismissively assessed by critic Leslie Halliwell thus:
'A former drug-dealer, who is being tempted to get involved in
one last major deal, and his friend, an undercover narcotics cop,
compete for the same girl.'

But once *Lethal Weapon* began to show its paces at the box
office Warners became determined to launch a much-hyped
sequel. They almost doubled Gibson's fee to $2.4 million,
secured Danny Glover's name on a new contract and added Joe
Pesci, Joss Ackland and Patsy Kensit to the cast. Even so the project might not have got off the ground so easily but for the high-
profile key figures off-camera.

Both director/producer Richard Donner and producer Joel
Silver were virtually in a class of their own in fast-paced adven-
ture pictures. Donner directed *The Omen, Superman* and *The
Goonies* as well as the original *Lethal Weapon*. Silver's record
over a period of seven years was equally impressive. He had
been involved with five high-grossing movies worldwide –
Forty-Eight Hours, Commando, Predator, Lethal Weapon and
Die Hard.

Gibson had been lukewarm about doing another *Lethal
Weapon*. He was not alone. Richard Donner was hesitant on
artistic grounds. 'In the past, when I'd finished either a feature
or a pilot for television, I'd felt that I had created something,
and the specific challenge of that project was over,' he said.
However, never fundamentally opposed to the idea of a *Lethal
Weapon* sequel, his first intention was to limit his involvement
and simply produce the film alongside Joel Silver. 'What ultimately happened,' he explained, 'was that as we became more
and more involved in the planning of the picture, and we got a
terrific script from Jeffrey Boam, I became increasingly possessive – of the characters, the cast and even the crew, to the point
of not wanting anyone else to direct the film.'

It was Donner's decision to direct *Lethal Weapon 2* which
assured the return of Mel Gibson and Danny Glover in the roles
of Riggs and Murtaugh. Said Gibson at the time:

13

There's no shortage of action films on the market and you can throw action at an audience until it's coming out of their ears, but that doesn't guarantee success. What made *Lethal Weapon* unique to the genre was that Dick Donner understands that action doesn't mean a thing unless the audience has access to it by really getting to know the characters first. Dick goes to great pains to set up the background in that way before he takes you on a roller-coaster ride.

Glover added, and Mel agreed, that working with the same team again made the new movie feel like a continuation, rather than a sequel. One of the new key elements in the second *Lethal Weapon* was highlighted by Gibson. 'Guys like Riggs are addicted to the adrenalin in their systems. They've lived a certain way for a long period of time and they don't like coming down. Although Riggs has gotten over his emotional problems he remains a man who lives close to the edge.' Richard Donner added: 'The change in Martin Riggs from *Lethal Weapon* to *Lethal Weapon* 2 is that now he stops to figure out the odds, because he wants to live.' Another important development was the introduction of humour, while the essential ingredients of spectacle and action were maintained.

But a follow-up to a successful film carries no guarantee of a second triumph at the box office, though most are made for that reason. The gamble in making *Lethal Weapon* 2, however, paid off in spectacular fashion. It roared to blockbuster status around the world, the US box office alone reaching $147 million, more than twice the takings of its predecessor.

But Mel Gibson was now ready to bury Martin Riggs, though his decision was considered by Warner Brothers as highly academic at the time because of *Lethal Weapon's* earlier successes. You could not go on milking the LA cop routine forever. Times change. Audiences become tired of the same routines and characters. Sure, *Mad Max* had gone into a third reincarnation, but that was exceptional – the exception that confirmed the rule.

Gibson turned his attention elsewhere. Pictures were making him rich and he had no thoughts of giving up the business. At thirty-three years old, he was now in his prime, with a devoted wife and growing family that he adored. Some areas of his life were highly disciplined. While he had become disillusioned with much of modern Catholicism, he still considered himself a devout Catholic in the sense of upholding the fundamental principles he had grown up with in his family home as a child. He was articulate, often deep-thinking and serious.

But he was also the inveterate joker, both on a film set and off. The inherent wild side of his character remained undisturbed. He could booze with the best of them. At one point his drinking became so worrying that his wife, Robyn, was said to have threatened to leave him if he did not give it up. 'I simply told him it could end our marriage and threaten his career,' she explained in a rare public statement.

She urged him to find help and secretly arranged for him to attend Alcoholics Anonymous, which he did, close to their luxury home in Malibu. It took enormous personal courage as a high-profile international star to attend these meetings. The drip-feed, one-day-at-a-time rehabilitation process was painful, slow and humiliating, but Robyn was always there to provide close and continuing support. Gibson's drinking began when he was still in his teens. The Australian sunshine and easy-going lifestyle, where drinking among young men had the feel of a competitive sport, was never likely to supply the self-discipline necessary to keep the bottle in check. Nor was his status as a rapidly ascending movie star. When the major film offers started to come in, leading to the purchase of a Hollywood home, it was even harder to control his intake. His intensive work programme piled on the pressure.

His own natural exuberant and joky personality did not help either. Another drink all round was natural, sociable and spontaneous. He admits that he found it difficult to come to terms with his huge success, achieved in just a few years after starring in *Mad Max*. It transformed his life. Working on location far from home, with long gaps in shooting, was often seen as the ideal opportunity to sink a few beers to break the monotony, though he retained an impeccable record of professionalism when working in front of the cameras.

After the crunch came and the battle began, Robyn and the children, whenever practicable, accompanied Mel to film locations all over the world. He found their presence reassuring, stabilizing and enormously supportive.

Overwork was another demon to be kept under control. His schedule during the 1980s had been one of the most punishing and potentially crippling in the whole of Hollywood, with many films being made on a hectic 'back-to-back' basis. Including the first *Mad Max* picture in 1980 and *Lethal Weapon 2* in 1989, no fewer than thirteen major pictures starring Gibson were released. It was an impressive output.

Brief interludes on his farm in northern Victoria, Australia, brought the chance to recharge his batteries and relax with his wife and children. Then it was back to his other world of movie-making, where the treadmill churned on inexorably.

He was keen to do a light-hearted comedy and grasped the chance when offered *Bird on a Wire* with the bubbly Goldie Hawn, released in 1990. The critics turned up their noses, blasting the picture but leaving the actors relatively unscathed. *Air America*, also out in 1990, was even less consequential, with Mel featured as an anti-hero. But *Hamlet* in 1991 more than made up for the previous year. Mel was suitably satisfied with his portrayal of the tortured prince battling with his sanity and his conscience to avenge his father's death. Some critics said it was his finest performance to date.

But among the cinema-going public Mel Gibson continued to be associated most closely with those enormously successful *Mad Max* and *Lethal Weapon* movies. It was now some four years since *Lethal Weapon* was released and only two since *Lethal Weapon 2* had set the screen ablaze. Mel had already made it clear that he was not interested in dragging it out once again.

Warner Brothers had other ideas. Mel Gibson was now their number one star. He was one of the biggest draws in the whole of Hollywood and was likely to remain so for many years to come. Fearing he might be tempted to defect elsewhere, the studio's major concern was to secure his future with them. Yet towards the end of 1990 the bigger studios were intent on bringing down budgets. Along with Gibson, only Kevin Costner and Tom Cruise, perhaps Julia Roberts also, could command fees in excess of $5 million for a picture.

The general tightening of belts continued into 1991. It was against these prevailing financial cutbacks in the major studios that Warners staggered Hollywood with a remarkable offer which even surprised Gibson. In February 1991 the star's lawyers were able to finalize an astonishing deal: four Mel Gibson movies in exchange for $42 million, with the promise of a lucrative additional arrangement which would also see the star benefit from a share in the profits of each picture. His advisers estimated that he could earn around $100 million from the package which also – for Mel – guaranteed him a three months' break from filming each year to spend with his wife and family.

With such a deal secured it is hardly surprising that Warners, too, got what they wanted. *Lethal Weapon 3* was made with Gibson in the starring role, and their strategy paid off handsomely. The picture grossed $160 million at the American box office alone and Mel became a $10 million man for the first time . . . his basic fee for the picture.

1   Six out of Ten

In the worldwide scheme of things you might be hard pressed to carve out a special place for Peekskill, in upper New York State, however predisposed you might feel towards the place. West Point, site of the famous US Military Academy, admittedly is not too far away. More distant to the north is the Catskill mountain range, associated with Rip Van Winkle, the fictional character of American diplomat and writer Washington Irving. Yet it was at the local hospital at Peekskill, at 4.45 p.m. on Tuesday, 3 January 1956, that Hutton Peter Mylott Gibson and his wife, Anne, closed their eyes and quietly gave thanks to the Lord for the safe arrival of a healthy son.

Peekskill was thereby placed on the map forever. For the infant who was christened Mel Columbcille (pronounced Columkille) Gerard just eleven days later at the imposing St Patrick's Church that overlooks the historic and pleasant town of Verplanck, where the Gibson family had their home, was destined to become one of the film industry's biggest superstars and the town's most famous son.

Hutton and Anne were staunch Catholics dedicated to raising a large and loving family and a new birth was not an altogether novel experience for them. Patricia, Sheila, Mary B. (Bridget), Kevin (Bernard) and Maura (Louise) had all safely entered the world before Mel's celebrated arrival. Identical twins Danny (Daniel Leo) and Chris (Christopher Stuart), Donal (Regis Gerard) and Ann were to follow. And if ten children were not enough, thirteen years later in 1969, Hutton and Anne would adopt Andrew with the same degree of enthusiasm which had attended the birth of their own biological brood. Then even the Gibsons declared that eleven children were enough!

Back in 1956 their choice of names for their latest addition – Mel was not a shortened version of any other name, incidentally – raised an eyebrow or two even among people who knew them best. It has long since passed into the Gibson family folklore that at the baptism, when a very close friend heard those names read out for the first time, his eyes opened wide and he simply could not believe what he heard. Later he joked that Mel was likely to be attending high school or college before he would know how to spell his own name.

The children grew up in a God-fearing, disciplined household where traditional values always counted more than domestic expediency and material gain. Before she married Hutton Gibson, Mel's mother was Anne Patricia Reilly, whose family lived on Granite Street in the heart of the predominantly Irish and German community in the Bushwick district of Brooklyn, the heavily populated borough of New York City located to the south-east of Manhattan. Of proud Irish stock, Anne would almost certainly have been born in her mother's adopted America but for a curious twist of fate. Her maternal grandmother, a widow suffering indifferent health, still lived in a pleasant country district in County Longford in Southern Ireland. Despite being heavily pregnant, Anne's mother decided she must visit her ailing mother and it was while she was in Ireland that Anne was born.

The year was 1921. Mother and new daughter returned to the United States and Anne attended the local school in the parish of Our Lady of Lourdes, later to graduate from a public school, Bushwick High. Showing creative talent she attended art school in Manhattan, after which, while still living with her parents in Brooklyn, she worked on Seventh Avenue, near Pennsylvania Station, developing and printing photographs.

The family background of the man she would eventually marry contrasts sharply in many ways with Anne's own life during those early years. It began many years before when a young, ambitious and adventurous Eva Mylott left her family in Australia to seek her fortune as an opera singer in the United States.

It was an exhausting, insecure existence with all the uncertainties and temptations which a stage career in those days entailed. There were boyfriends and liaisons as she trekked from

19

one venue to another to appear in concerts, but nothing which seemed very serious to her. Nothing, that is, until she met, fell in love with and married a millionaire steel executive named John Hutton Gibson. It was the first time in her life that she was able to enjoy any lasting stability and security.

Despite her previously exciting, always-on-the-move, colourful lifestyle, Eva settled immediately to domesticity and was a caring and loving wife. Marriage brought her a deep and inner satisfaction she had not known before. Though comfortably settled in a fine house in Mountclair in New York State, she retained an affection for her home country and cared about its implicated plight as Europe headed for confrontation. After the declaration of war in 1914 she helped to raise money to send medical supplies to her native Australia.

Domestically, only one important feature was missing from her life. She had no children, though she longed to be a mother. At age forty-three in 1918, and against strong medical advice because of her age, Eva now became pregnant and was delighted when she gave birth to a healthy son (Mel's father), whom they christened Hutton Peter. She and her husband's happiness was now complete, but deeper concerns were expressed when she quickly became pregnant again, giving birth to a second son, Alexander Mylott. Fears for Eva's health grew with the rapid onset of serious post-natal complications and, once she was aware that her condition was terminal, Eva found happiness and contentment in the knowledge that the Gibson name would live on. Within a few weeks of her young son's birth, she died, long before her natural time, and was buried in Chicago.

John Hutton Gibson was inconsolable. His deep love for his late wife made remarriage an impossible option. He engaged a housekeeper to look after his sons until they were old enough to attend the local school in Rockford, Illinois. It was at this point that the seed of religion was implanted deeply in the conscience of Eva's distraught widower, a legacy which would be inherited unquestioningly by his son, Hutton Peter (Mel's father), and indeed later by Mel himself.

To ease the pain of his enormous personal loss John Hutton Gibson turned to the Roman Catholic Church. It was a faith which kept him going during the black months of his deep mourning and also during a second devastation in his life when the Great Depression of the 1930s broke through his once comfortable and seemingly impregnable financial position. His flourishing business collapsed and by the time his sons were finishing high school the family fortune was virtually gone. Young Hutton Peter, his first-born son, inherited those deeply religious family instincts and later entered a seminary to study to be a priest. He was an uncompromising individual who saw right and wrong in clearly defined, indisputable terms. His personal discipline was absolute. But after two years he decided the priesthood was not for him after all.

After the death of his father and the beginning of World War Two, Hutton Gibson decided to enlist in the US Infantry. It was the first significant move on the way to meeting his future wife. For Hutton was sent to Fort Benning in Georgia for his basic training, there becoming friendly with Harold Cardello, a fellow GI, whose home was in Brooklyn. In those galvanizing, all-pull-together wartime days it was not unusual to be invited to a buddy's home when leave was due. Hutton eagerly accepted Harold's invitation and travelled with him to his home.

It was at this point that circumstances contrived to bring Mel's mother and father together. Cardello had worked in the Flatbush section of the Brooklyn transit authority. His close friend there had recently married Kathleen Reilly, Anne Patricia Reilly's older sister, and it was through his visits to Kathleen's home that Hutton Gibson met Anne Reilly. They enjoyed one another's company almost from the moment they met, though in a subdued kind of way. She was a kind, gentle and pleasant girl from a loving and considerate home, genuine in her relationships and intelligent, though not as worldly or knowledgeable as Hutton.

Unlike many wartime romances which quickly reached flashpoint, Mel's mother's and father's relationship developed slowly, but genuinely. Hutton was never impulsive or impetuous, his motives and actions always controlled by his deep religious instincts and beliefs. But as they met more often it became obvious that they were increasingly attracted to each other. Years later Mel's Aunt Kathleen 'went public' on these early love-kindling days. 'We always knew Hutton as Red because of his red hair,' she recalled. 'He wasn't at all outgoing; he seemed shy and distant and could make you feel a bit uncomfortable at first. But

21

once you got to know him he was a very warm person.'

When Hutton Gibson moved to nearby Fort Monmouth, New Jersey, as an officer candidate in the Signal Corps, his visits to Kathleen's home became more frequent. Even then he showed his instinctive love of family life and would make himself at home, playing with Kathleen's children in a genuinely spontaneous and enjoyable way. Meantime the relationship between Hutton and Anne continued to develop steadily, if quietly, and they surprised no one when they became engaged.

But soon they were parted. As a second lieutenant Mel's father saw service overseas and was finally sent home after being wounded in the Battle of Guadalcanal. Then on Monday morning, 1 May 1944, Mel's mother and father were married in a simple ceremony at the Church of Our Lady of Good Counsel in Brooklyn.

By then Hutton worked for the New York Central Railroad in a job which paid above average for those times and they lived comfortably in an apartment in Manhattan. Both Hutton and Anne had declared their intention of wanting a large family and it was on 1 April the following year, just eleven months after their marriage, that Patricia was born, when Anne was twenty-four. No parents could have been prouder or more delighted.

But as more babies quickly followed, the Gibsons outgrew their Manhattan home, first moving thirty miles north to the small quiet community of Croton-on-Hudson and then again to Verplanck, one of a number of villages on the east bank of the Hudson River, settling into a compact, pleasant, if noisy, single-storey home close to the entrance to the Sun Oil Company depot, with its regular in-and-out traffic of tanker trucks, day and night.

As the family grew, Hutton's spare time was filled with repeated and necessary extensions to the house. Even so the family quickly seemed to expand to fill it. The special sense of community and belonging which members of large families often seem to enjoy was certainly a feature of the Gibson household. Neighbours and friends who recall those days talk of the house being full of children. Mel remembered many years later his strict upbringing in a happy, disciplined home, where the increasingly tempting excesses of changing times were firmly held in check. For a long time there was no television. The

22

cheaper and nastier comic books were banned. There were toys for the children to play with, but nothing expensive or extravagant. Those were not the yardsticks of fun, happiness and contentment in the Gibson homestead. The children were encouraged to make their own entertainment and the young Mel soon began to show himself to be a happy, outgoing, fun-loving individual. Even then he was prone to playing tricks and fooling around, though according to an obviously adoring Aunt Kathleen many years later, he was never a bad boy.

Both Hutton and Anne considered it their responsibility to set a good example to their children in terms of attitude and behaviour. For both of them the family was omnipotent, a philosophy which they steadfastly handed down to their children. All the youngsters were encouraged to value the simple pleasures of life, rather than grow to depend on expensively bought items of fleeting enjoyment. Worldly possessions were not the answer to a happy and fulfilled life. It was perhaps a throw-back to these early formative times when many years later, after he had become a Hollywood megastar and was confronted by the tedious question 'What's it like being very, very rich?', Mel's flippant and impatient response was: 'Money gives you the freedom to do really stupid things with your time.'

The Gibsons were known locally not solely for the size of their family, but also for their Christian and neighbourly way of life. They seldom socialized. Hutton was a pillar of the local Catholic church which the family attended regularly and where Hutton exercised his fine baritone voice in the choir. Their days were centred on the family, school and the church. Family holidays were too expensive and therefore non-existent. Birthdays were never missed, but mostly celebrated quietly within the home with some of Anne's special cakes.

Hutton set the ground rules for his family's standards, conduct and way of life. He was the unchallenged head of the household. The regime was strict and everyone was required to stick to it. He worked the night shift on the railroad and was a conscientious employee. Anne therefore spent most of her time looking after the family and tending to the children's almost never-ending needs. She was a loving and contented wife and mother with a reputation for home cooking and renowned for 'keeping a good table' – perhaps a little too good when set against today's standards of healthy eating. For in those days carefully balanced, healthy diets were uncommon, if not unknown, though Hutton himself was said to be extremely health-conscious, insisting that his family join him in taking vit-amin pills every day. According to Mel many years later, his mother's speciality was Irish soda bread flan with raisins. 'There was also plenty of stews, pies and hot-pots,' he added. 'We always had enough to eat.'

Hutton Gibson was a knowledgeable man and quite capable, many folk believed, of holding down a better, more highly-paid job. But he appeared content to remain with the railroad com-pany where his loyalty, dedication and ability were rewarded with a number of promotions over the years. He was by no means a willing or instinctive spender, finding more satisfaction in watching his savings build steadily against the day when he could move his family into a better and more spacious home.

That day arrived in spring 1961. The Gibsons had lived in Verplanck for eleven years and Mel was five years old when Hutton's latent ambition finally surfaced to surprise his friends and neighbours. He had now enough money put aside to move house and confidently took the family further north and across the river to Mount Vision. The Gibson's fine new home was a handsome, spacious farmhouse with an outbuilding or two and surrounded by land which Hutton calculated was big enough, given time, to build up into a profitable concern.

Meantime, Mel's father continued with his job on the rail-road, though it made for a committed and arduous lifestyle which left him little time to spend with his family. He drove his ancient station-wagon to his work base at Croton-Harmon at the start of every working week and would stay in the city, often sleeping at his in-laws in New York, until it was time to drive back to his idyllic, rural retreat for weekends spent happily with his family.

But Hutton considered the sacrifice worth while. The new home gave all the family much more space than there had been at Verplanck and near-total freedom out-of-doors to wander through the large garden and play contentedly in the fields. They could walk, boat, fish, even swim when the weather was right, without restriction. It was an isolated spot, and with Hutton away for much of the week Anne spent a lot of time on her own with the children. But they had plenty of visitors, relatives from the city and friends from where they lived previously. The farmhouse was sufficiently large and had enough rooms for many of the visitors to stay overnight in comfort. With an eye to adding to the family income Hutton bought a few head of beef cattle, though he knew little enough about them. But the children loved to have them around. A special celebration held at Mount Vision was the birth of their tenth and last baby, Ann.

Along with the rest of the family, the young Mel Gibson enjoyed the natural freedoms of their new home. It probably gave him a life-long taste for the unrestricted nature of farm life which, many years later when Hollywood made him rich, he revelled in once again after buying farms in Australia and America which could be enjoyed by his own large family – though as a child, rumour has it, he did what he could to avoid cleaning out the cattle pens. But he was still young then, young enough to remain at home with his mother when the older children started their new school.

One concern for Hutton was the absence of a Catholic school nearby, so the older children attended the local public Central School in Laurens, just a few miles south. Old man Gibson is still distantly remembered there for the way he tried to increase and influence the school's religious syllabus. At the same time all his children were required to continue their religious studies and development diligently in their own time at home.

The Gibsons soon acquired a reputation for their willing and wholehearted participation in school activities. Mel celebrated his sixth birthday in January 1962 and in the following September joined his older brother Kevin and (Patricia having recently graduated) his sisters Sheila, Mary B. and Maura on the school bus each day. He was considered a bright youngster by his teacher. He went through first, second and third grades at the Laurens school. Still the most celebrated picture in the school archives to this day, perhaps, shows a smiling Mel Gibson posing with third-grade classmates, three girls and seven boys. Then on Sunday, 7 October 1962, Mel received his first Holy Communion at the small Holy Cross Catholic Church in the nearby community of Morris.

Where the Gibsons lived was indeed a beautiful place and the family loved it, but like so many idealistic visions, their personal Shangri-La was to prove unsustainable. For one thing the area chosen by Hutton proved to be less consistently fertile than he had anticipated, the winter snows reducing the farming season to just three months. Another problem developed in winter when the water in the spring up in the mountains and on which they depended for their household needs, was frozen over for weeks on end. Reluctantly, Hutton had to admit that the homestead was never going to be a viable proposition commercially.

By this time he had also discovered that the area around where they lived was predominantly Protestant. The local antipathy towards the Catholic Church was not helped by a number of other large Catholic families who had moved into the area. Those who were born and bred there and regarded the area as their natural home began to feel uneasy, if not exactly threatened, by the Catholic infiltration.

Hutton was practical enough to realize that some important decisions for the future of his family would have to be made. He was running out of money, but some extraordinary events, disconnected and separated in time, were to take place that claimed the initiative and dramatically changed the Gibsons' lives forever. Had they not taken place, who knows . . . Mel Gibson might never have found his way to Hollywood.

The first unexpected event shattered the family's contented and stable routine. Approaching the end of his shift down the railroad yard, Hutton was aboard engine number 8595 when he slipped on some oil deposits and fell heavily, sustaining severe back injuries. By the time Anne received the shock news back at the Mount Vision farm, just before dawn on Friday 11 December 1964, Hutton had been rushed to hospital with a suspected broken back. X-rays later revealed severe spinal injuries, which included herniated lumbar discs. Painful treatment, incorporating a series of delicate operations, followed. The whiplash effects of the accident were also responsible for the onset of arthritis and degenerative changes.

It was the end of Hutton's working life on the railroad. During the painful months of recuperation and rehabilitation the family shared Hutton's anguish as he battled for compensation from the railroad. New York Central refused to admit liability and the case dragged on. Meantime, it was not financially possible to continue living in their present home. Having placed their Mount Vision farm on the market, the family moved south and into an old rambling, tumbledown property at Salisbury Mills, just across the river from Verplanck. It couldn't match the farm at Mount Vision in the family's affections, but, more importantly then, it was available at a peppercorn rent.

Times were hard. While never ambitious for the luxuries of life, the family's focus was now very much on survival. Friends and relatives helped as much as they could, but it was a grim situation. Two of Mel's older sisters, now finished high school, took jobs to help boost the family income. But Hutton's faith in God and a better future for them all never wavered.

Mel and the younger children now attended school in Washingtonville, a delightful village three miles west. And it was here that all the family were regular attenders at St Mary's Catholic Church. It was a proud occasion for them all when on Saturday, 22 May 1965, the nine-year-old Mel was confirmed there, for in addition, Mel's eldest sister Patricia and brother Kevin had both only recently told the family that they were entering religious orders – Patricia as a novice at a convent near Albany and Kevin to a seminary near Newburgh.

Shortly after, a further significant event took place which contributed to an upsurge in the Gibson family fortunes. Hutton had filled his physically inactive time following his accident with a rigorous self-imposed programme of reading and learning but then, applying his mind to the need to bolster the family finances, he remembered how he had once won a few hundred dollars in a local television quiz programme. At the time *Jeopardy* was a TV show in New York City which gave big cash prizes to successful contestants. Encouraged by his family, Hutton sent off a letter and was accepted on the show.

It was a nail-biting experience, but Hutton was well up to the challenge, answering one question after another to win several thousand dollars. More importantly, his success gained him automatic entry into the championship run-off. And that is exactly what Hutton did – run off with the top prize in the championship, a cheque for $21,000.

His success proved timely, for it seems the family were on the verge of being evicted from their home for not being able to pay even the minimal rent. Hutton's high-profile triumph was an enormous boost to the family, lifting their spirits and re-estab-

27

lishing their confidence. By this time even Hutton Gibson had acknowledged that times were changing, at least to the extent of having a small-screen, black-and-white television in the home. Mel was there with his mother and the other members of the family crowded round the set, yelling and cheering repeatedly as Hutton continued to come up with the right answers.

This good fortune was followed by another windfall when Hutton's legal battle with the railroad company was finally settled. It had been a tortuous journey through the courts, lasting more than three wearisome years, and there were still seven more days of critical uncertainty once the case came to trial at Westchester County Court House in White Plains. Then on Wednesday, 14 February 1968, Hutton was awarded $145,000 by the court. His lawyers were disappointed in the size of the settlement, but Hutton was philosophical. Even after paying his legal fees more than enough money remained to settle his outstanding debts.

And after that? Hutton Peter Mylott Gibson was already well on the way to making the biggest decision of his life – a decision which would change the life of a not-yet-teenage Mel Gibson and that of his mother and all his brothers and sisters.

2 Early Days in Oz

Hutton Gibson had plenty of time to contemplate the world during his lengthy battle to regain his health. Much of what he saw distressed and angered him. Old values he had inherited and upheld without question were flagrantly being swept aside. The solid framework and self-discipline which had given deep-rooted purpose to his own life, and that of his family, were under attack. 'Flower power', a startling manifestation of these changing times, had rocked his sensibilities. He was having to live with the more excessive freedoms of the swinging sixties, and was fearful that society as a whole was in danger of being sucked in to the extremes of a new and increasingly pervasive sub-culture of youth.

Equally disturbing to Hutton Gibson was the conduct of the United States in world events. While it is likely that he would have welcomed the inauguration of John Fitzgerald Kennedy as his country's first Roman Catholic president in 1961, he was perhaps much less pleased at a personal level by his decision to involve the United States in the Vietnam War. Hutton's concerns grew after Lyndon Johnson, who became president after Kennedy's assassination, increased his country's military involvement in Vietnam. A pacifist by inclination, he witnessed with alarm the American administration's deepening commitment to the far-flung battle against communism.

But long before the strength of public opposition in the United States forced President Nixon into reopening negotiations for peace, a disillusioned and alarmed Hutton Gibson had made the decision that would radically change the lives of all his family. After his experience in World War Two he had vowed never to let his children face the possibility of death or serious

29

injury in a similar conflict. In 1968 young Mel was only twelve years old and safe for a while, but his older brother Kevin would soon be eligible for the draft. It was enough to convince Hutton that his decision was right and well-timed. They would emigrate and start a new life in his mother's native Australia.

Hutton was intellectually well equipped for the new challenge. When recovering from his accident he had attended a rehabilitation centre in Newburgh, New York State, for guidance in selecting a new career. The results of his IQ tests gave him a remarkable 'genius' rating and he was advised to train as a programmer in the new and fast developing business of computers. This he did. He was also able to finance the move to Australia from his accident compensation and television winnings. In fact in a conspicuously expansive gesture he decided his family deserved a holiday and arranged a series of stop-overs which added up to a mini world tour.

Hutton Gibson thought long and hard before deciding to move to Australia. He talked his plans over with Anne, and all members of the family were consulted and encouraged to have their say. It was a major step which would affect all their lives and so strong were the Gibson family ties that Patricia and Kevin immediately withdrew from their religious orders to travel with the party. Hutton refused to be overawed by the logistical complications of getting himself, his wife and ten children more than half-way round the world. The final day in their home country was spent with Aunt Kathleen at a picnic lunch at her home outside New York. Then they left America behind, on 4 July (Independence Day) 1968, making first for Ireland and Scotland, then England, Switzerland and Italy, finally visiting Rome and the Vatican. Being in the Vatican was a very special experience for the Gibsons and, as committed Roman Catholics, they spent a good deal of their time in prayer. They also enjoyed the bustle and informality of Rome and its pavement cafés, chattering crowds and, of course, its long cultural history.

The Gibsons spent time in Perth and Adelaide before arriving in Melbourne. The *Melbourne Herald* of 4 November 1968 greeted their arrival with the headline: 'Welcome the Gibsons – all 12 of them.' The accompanying 'team' photograph shows a bright twelve-year-old Mel Gibson, in open-necked shirt and sports jacket, alongside Daniel and Christopher (11), Donal (10) and Ann (7). Seated in front are Mr and Mrs Gibson with Patricia (23), Sheila (21), Mary (20), Kevin (18) and Maura (14). Hutton Gibson, at the end of the row, looks relaxed while his wife, Anne, comes across as rather ample and jolly-looking.

After Hutton had investigated the main cities he decided to settle his family in Sydney, even then a bustling metropolis. After the fierce winters at their homes in New York State, the warmth and brilliant sunshine of Australia was a welcome and exciting contrast. They looked in awe across Sydney's magnificent harbour and could hardly wait to visit the city's famous Bondi Beach. Hutton found a house in Mount Kuring-gai, just north of the city, and the younger children were settled into schools. Mel attended St Leo's College, set in the pleasant suburb of Wahroonga and close to desirable and expensive properties. More to the point for Hutton was that St Leo's was run by a group of Catholic priests who maintained strict standards and a highly disciplined routine.

While Mel was familiar with strict discipline, he had not expected the relentless and often cruel banter and abuse from his schoolmates. Poking fun at his American accent, they made sure this new-boy upstart was kept in his place, though at this time Mel was quiet and somewhat shy. When provoked into fighting in self-defence and to uphold his standing in the school, he would then become the target for further punishment from his teachers, who soon had him marked down as a troublemaker. He kept to himself as much as possible and found little consolation in sports like cricket and football which he had never played and knew nothing about. He reacted by needling his teachers. He acquired among his peers a dubious reputation which meant that his teachers clamped down all the harder. Mel confessed many years later: 'I hated that school.'

He admitted that he wasted much of his time trying to get even with the teachers and gradually his natural exuberance, his capacity for fun and playing jokes became irrepressible. His theatrical pratfalls were executed to a high standard and extremely convincing to those around him. Teachers and pupils were shocked and alarmed when one moment he was standing there perfectly normally and the next he was collapsed in a heap at their feet. Education was passing Mel by, despite being really quite bright.

31

This dreary time ended, not because of Mel's misery, but when his father discovered that St Leo's was not matching up to his own standards for religious instruction. He was shocked to find that the pupils were not required to attend Mass every day. Uncompromising as always about religious instruction for his children, Hutton presented himself at St Leo's one day, told the priests what he thought of their policy, and took Mel out of the school. After that Mel was sent to a state school and was given regular religious instruction at home.

Asquith Boys High School turned out to be a much happier experience for the youngster. At first he was again pushed, bullied and teased because of his American accent and background, but this time Mel was not so easily intimidated and would quickly fight back. He soon settled down and gained respect among his classmates and staff and was reasonably popular. His American accent became less pronounced and he could be fun and entertaining to be around. Though basically shy, he loved to play the fool, setting up various pranks and playing around. It was at Asquith High that they christened him 'Mad Mel' after an eccentric disc jockey popular on Sydney radio. He was energetic and boisterous and did not always know just how far to take his fun-making. Ken Coleby was a senior prefect during Mel's days at Asquith High. 'We had to pull him into line several times a week at first,' he explained. 'Never for anything malicious because Mel wasn't like that. Mainly for crazy stunts he had pulled on unsuspecting people, teachers too sometimes.'

As a fifteen-year-old Mel Gibson was good-looking, energetic, with twinkling blue eyes. His boundless energy and outgoing attitude were not always appreciated by adults. His coordination was exceptional. He modelled his pratfalls on Peter Sellers and could do them with all the flair and precision of that celebrated British actor. Typical of his age, with hair dropping down to his shoulders, he delighted in causing surprise, consternation or embarrassment in public with some foolish stunts. There was no sense of malice in what he did. It was the reaction on victims' faces which most intrigued and delighted him.

Life at home continued to be tightly disciplined. Routines, attitudes and conduct were set in stone and based on fundamental Catholic doctrines and the ever-present example of his father. Hutton had settled into a good and well-paid job as a computer programmer, but with the family growing up there were fewer children around the house. Mel's mother, Anne, loved children and even back in America had promised herself that once they had arrived safely and were settled in Australia, she would love to adopt. They had been in Sydney little more than a year when nine-month-old Andrew joined the Gibson clan. He was their eleventh child.

Meantime Mel was growing up and being subjected increasingly to outside influences. He had responded with youthful vigour and enthusiasm to his new life in Australia, the sunshine, the carefree lifestyle, the surfing and the matey friendships. His deep love and respect for his parents remained as strong as ever. In the home he adhered to the rule book without question, kneeling for prayers three times daily. His knowledge of the Bible was impressive.

But Mel Gibson was also an average teenager and became a different person once outside the house. He was growing up and formulating his own ideas. He wanted to have fun and be one of the boys. He said that he was about fifteen when, away from home, he first started to smoke and drink beer; girls crept on to the agenda. In some ways outgoing, Mel was still basically shy. Girls noticed his good looks, even if he was uncomfortable in their company. A drink or two, at first secured illegally because he was under-age, boosted his confidence, and in the same year went on his first date – a girl he met while out drinking with his friends. They went to the movies, but according to Mel, nothing much happened and it was hardly an outrageous success. He was just too nervous.

Much later he would recall those awkward mid-teen years: 'I was never a womanizer. I didn't have the chat. I'd go all tongue-tied and embarrassed if a girl came near me.' But there was little doubt that young Mel Gibson was enjoying life in Australia. His father, however, expressed some concern about his son's future once schooldays were over. Mel admitted he did not know what he wanted to do. Fleetingly the idea of entering the church had in the past crossed his mind. Later he would spend three heavy, unrewarding months working in a bottle factory. He had thought casually about catering. Journalism was another vague notion, but the more he thought about it the less attractive it became.

Eye-witness to family talk about Mel's work possibilities was his older sister, Sheila. She had ideas of her own about brother Mel. His natural talent for playing the fool, the way he could pretend to be someone or do something, his keen portrayal of Scottish and other accents and his ability to throw himself to the floor without hurting himself suggested he might just have a future as an actor. He certainly loved the movies and spent many of his leisure hours in darkened picture houses enthralled by his favourite actor, Humphrey Bogart. But when confronted with the need to consider his future seriously he never contemplated acting. He said years later: 'I'd see Bogart doing something wonderfully adventurous and I'd think how great he was and wished I could be like him. But with the picture over and once more in the bright reality of day, I'd be back in the real world trying to decide my future.'

Sheila remembered how, while at St Leo's College, Mel had appeared on stage, taking the part of a villain in a school melodrama. Convinced he would never seriously consider trying to become a professional actor, Sheila secretly took the initiative herself, aiming high. On her brother's behalf she sent off an application to the prestigious National Institute of Dramatic Art (NIDA) at the University of New South Wales in Sydney. It was an extremely long shot because even at that time NIDA had been responsible for nurturing some of Australia's best and most successful talent. They did not accept just anyone.

When Sheila told Mel what she had done he was neither excited nor annoyed. He showed little more emotion when he was called for an audition. Once there, though gripped with nerves, his readings from *King Lear* and *Death of a Salesman* obviously showed promise for he passed the audition, becoming one of only twenty students selected that year, scores more hopefuls being turned away. He did not exactly enjoy his early days at NIDA. He was still nervous, yet somehow had the feeling that he ought to persevere. So anxious was he in his first play, it is said, that he was unable to stand and had to play the part sitting down. Yet there was a fascination, a kind of bewitching, seductive attraction in acting which he found compulsive. Almost subconsciously he felt a commitment to carry on.

Meantime others were forming judgements. Mel was cast in a student production of *Romeo and Juliet*. The play was directed by Richard Wherrett, who later commented: 'I knew from the first that Mel was on his way to becoming a star, but he was very shy.' Tutors who guided him as a fledgling actor talked about his difficulties in breaking down the barriers of inhibition, which made him feel uncomfortable and tense on stage. 'It was something like a year before I started to like or enjoy acting,' Mel explained. 'Finally, NIDA was like another little world that I got lost in for those years.'

That student production of *Romeo and Juliet* was memorable for Gibson because he played opposite another future screen star, Judy Davis. Two years later they would appear together again, this time in a professional production of the same play, at Sydney's Nimrod Theatre. The same age as Gibson, but born in Australia, Davis dropped out of convent school to sing in a rock band before making her name in pictures. They were kindred souls at NIDA, sharing the same fears and hopes, and their friendship continued over the years. Davis went on to gain international recognition a little ahead of Gibson, in 1979, with Gillian Armstrong's Australian movie, *My Brilliant Career*. Later came *Who Dares Wins*, the SAS thriller, in 1982, and two years later, *A Passage to India*, written and directed by David Lean, in which she starred alongside the established talent of Alec Guinness, Peggy Ashcroft, James Fox and Nigel Havers, and for which she received an Academy Award nomination. Years later Davis confirmed that in their days at NIDA Mel 'sent up' the balcony scene in *Romeo and Juliet*. 'He made his Adam's apple very big and gulped loudly, which got a big laugh,' she explained.

According to Gibson himself there was no instant flash of realization which suggested he could make a success of acting; even less that he could make a living from it. 'There was a time when certain things began to make sense,' he explained. Many years later when asked the same kind of question he would simply say that acting gave him enormous pleasure. 'I don't do it because it gives me a chance to change the world or anything grand like that.' Others would point to another milestone, when he ceased to be scared out of his wits on stage and began to enjoy himself. That is when he really began to make remarkable strides as an actor and his enthusiasm soared. Keith Bain, his movement coach at NIDA, said it was impossible to cast him in a small part because he would just take over the play. It appears that it was only in the third and final year that Mel really applied himself seriously to his studies. Before that he was said to be more interested in having a good time. Only later did he become ambitious and determined to get on.

In those early days at NIDA Gibson was still something of the joking prankster, hiding his true feelings and, superficially at any rate, not prepared to take life too seriously. This made him wonder, his first year's training completed, if he would be invited to continue for a second year. Almost half the students fell at this hurdle, but Mel was more than a little surprised to find he was to be allowed to carry on. The more focused Judy Davis was also selected to continue her training.

By now Mel Gibson sported a beard to go with his shoulder-length hair and he relished the new-found freedoms enjoyed by young people. He felt the need to be more independent. Until now it had been convenient and enjoyable to travel to and from NIDA daily with attractive 18-year-old fellow student Linda Newton from their respective family homes in the upper north shore area of Sydney. But during the summer recess he told his parents that he felt the need to strike out on his own. The news was not exactly welcomed enthusiastically at home, but Hutton and Anne were sensible and responsible parents and appreciated their son's decision. After all, Mel was not the first of their children to grow up.

Back for another term, NIDA was hardly the most welcoming of places. At that time it was simply a collection of extremely basic, pre-fabricated huts, some of which had sprung leaks. But the training there was invaluable for a young, burgeoning actor and in any case Mel was excited by his new-found freedom, for by this time he was sharing a flat with a former class-mate from the dreaded St Leo's College, his old school of which he still had so many lingering and painful memories. The flat was situated in the cosmopolitan district of Kings Cross, a Sydney equivalent of London's Soho, with bars, restaurants, nightclubs, porn shops and other distractions. Mel was excited by the idea of living in the midst of all the action, but after a while found life in Kings Cross too hectic.

He moved into a run-down house close to Bondi Beach, sharing with Steve Bisley, a friend and fellow student at NIDA, and a couple of others of about the same age. Life was hectic, but exciting. There was a kind of one-day-at-a-time, colourful and cavalier pattern to their existence. Though in theory they shared the chores, the house was a tip. Money was scarce and they mostly lived close to the breadline. It was a hand-to-mouth existence and the young Mel and his crowd would stretch their meagre budget by 'sampling' items from a nearby fruit and veg stall. They were an energetic crowd and widely popular. Invitations to parties and free lunches or dinners were snapped up with relish. It was a time for stretching your experiences. Sydney was a lively, energetic city and the bright lights of the many bars were a big draw for young people out for an evening's fun and relaxation.

Mel continued his training at NIDA and was steadily becoming noticed for all the right reasons. Fellow students and staff began talking about his natural talent. He appeared to be more positive and ambitious; more comfortable on stage and more relaxed. And he worked hard. For the first time he seemed concerned to build a career. Mel was still attending NIDA when he was invited to make his first movie, a low-budget, fairly inconsequential affair which would not gain a general release outside Australia.

He was still in his final year at drama school when approached by Sydney's notable showbiz agents Faith Martin and Bill Shanahan. They saw him as a potential major talent and began lining up work for him. He did a two-week stint on the old Aussie soap opera, *The Sullivans*. The treadmill of daily screen appearances, insufficient time to rehearse and what he considered to be shallow storylines forced him to question his wisdom in allowing himself to be persuaded into television so early in his career. But the money was important.

During his few remaining months at NIDA he decided he was more interested in live theatre than the more detached worlds of film and television. He graduated as Bachelor of Dramatic Art from the National Institute, University of New South Wales in 1977 and thought he would concentrate on the stage for a while. He appeared at Sydney's Nimrod Theatre and toured with the South Australian Theatre Company, enjoying excellent reviews for his performance as Estragon in Beckett's *Waiting for Godot*. Appearing with Gibson in 1979 in a NIDA production of this

Beckett play was struggling fellow actor and one-time flat-mate, Geoffrey Rush. 'It was a magical cooperation,' said director George Whaley. But while Mel's career would soon take off with the success of *Mad Max* in 1980, Rush had to wait many more years for film recognition, with three consecutive roles in eighteen months, in *On Our Selection, Shine* and *Children of the Revolution*.

It was while appearing on stage in Adelaide that a chance meeting took place which would substantially change Mel's life. He was looking for a room to rent and followed up an advertisement. Robyn Moore, a young and attractive brunette who was already living in the flat, opened the door and showed him round. The place served his purpose well and at just $A15 a week on a shared tenancy basis, he could not do better.

Robyn was a dental nurse, reportedly a little shy in those days. In any event, the shared arrangement was strictly platonic for Robyn already had a boyfriend. As flatmates Mel and Robyn got along very well. She was from a secure, caring family and the pair were relaxed and comfortable in each other's company. 'We used to do things like going shopping together,' explained Mel some years later. In the end there was no room left for the boyfriend in Robyn and Mel's steadily growing relationship.

However, this development did not instantly increase the pace or intensity of their romance. Robyn had heard about actors and their unreliability as they moved around from place to place. She was instinctively cautious anyway. In the end the blossoming romance fulfilled its early promise and two years after their first meeting, in a quiet ceremony at a Catholic Church in Sydney in October 1980, Robyn Denise Moore, spinster of that parish, became Mrs Mel Columbcille Gerard Gibson. The partnership flourished and endured and in the end, produced six well-loved children.

But hold on. We are moving ahead far too quickly. First we need to look at that inauspicious film debut of Mel Gibson, then a novice actor and a national unknown but, as it would turn out, Australia's global superstar of the future.

3 First Steps to Fame

The twenty-year-old Mel Gibson was half-way through his three-year drama course at Sydney's National Institute of Dramatic Art, looking forward to the summer recess, when at a picturesque coastal location some 80 miles to the north, Phillip Avalon was given the crisis news. Nick Papadopoulous, a young actor he had in mind for the part of Scollop in his forthcoming film, *Summer City*, had pulled out of the running because of personal problems.

It was news he could well have done without, even though Scollop was not a lead part. The project, Avalon's first stab at film production, was already a nightmare. Not that he was looking for a commercial blockbuster. He never saw *Summer City* as anything more than an entertaining surfing film for showing at clubs and rented halls along the coast. Even so, raising the minuscule budget was not proving easy. He had started by taking as many odd jobs as he could find and buying and selling cars. He had already written the screenplay and cast himself in one of the parts. Unashamedly he pushed friends hard for contributions and pursued all would-be benefactors with zeal.

But Avalon saw his major economy coming from his ability to recruit young, talented actors who were even more desperate for the experience than for the money. In this way he could keep the payroll down and could slash expenses by providing only basic, make-shift accommodation during the scheduled three weeks of location work. Yet he would courageously start shooting the picture – economically, in 16mm format – with a big financial hole in the kitty still waiting to be filled. He had barely enough funds to cover the cost of the film stock he required and its processing.

Against this background Avalon took the news of Papadopoulous's enforced defection philosophically, especially when one of the cast, John Jarrat, said he knew an actor from NIDA who would be an ideal replacement. Jarrat had the young and unknown Mel Gibson in mind and on his recommendation Avalon agreed to visit NIDA to see Gibson during rehearsals. But pressured by other problems Avalon never made it. Jarrat, anxious himself for commercial reasons to see the film start shooting as quickly as possible, persisted and took Mel over to Avalon's home. It was hardly an audition. The producer looked him over for a few moments and muttered that he seemed about right for the supporting role of Scollop. 'Can't afford to pay much, though,' claimed Avalon, who never disguised the fact that it was only a little beach movie he was planning. 'Only a hundred dollars a week, for three weeks' work.' But later Gibson disputed the figure even going on to say that Avalon never paid him anyway. Avalon firmly denied the allegation.

But at the time almost any money would have been good enough for Mel. Another bonus was that Steve Bisley, then his closest friend, was also to appear in the picture, in the more important role of Boo. Making the picture would be fun and Mel figured it was a good enough way of making some spending money during the summer break from drama school. The deal was clinched when he was told that there were certain to be plenty of girls mooning around during shooting.

Phil Avalon had chosen Catherine Hill Bay, a small coastal mining village south of Newcastle, New South Wales, and about a one-hour drive north of Sydney, as the location for the picture. Mel and Steve Bisley received his permission to go up there a week early to get the feel of things, hitching a lift with Avalon, who also needed to be at the location ahead of time. They were to travel up in Avalon's old big, black Chevrolet which would also feature in the film; it would also become the scene of one of Gibson's earliest reported adventures as a do-as-you-please, freedom-loving young man of his time.

Mel had already noticed that the car was not legally registered when he discovered there was no petrol in the tank either. The first problem they could comfortably ignore. The car wasn't his anyway, though he was probably sailing close to the wind if he decided to do some of the driving. But having no petrol was certainly a problem because, first, they had precious little cash between them and, second, more money would have been no use anyway since petrol was virtually unobtainable in the Sydney area at that time because of an industrial dispute. So they set out to 'borrow' fuel from other cars in the vicinity of Avalon's home at the seaside resort of Tamarama.

Avalon later explained what happened next. 'Close to my home on the coast a car had rolled over a cliff. The police and ambulance services had been and gone, and we knew the tow-truck wasn't expected to haul up the crashed car until morning. So Mel and Steve climbed down with the gear they needed and milked enough fuel from the overturned car to cover the journey to Catherine Hill Bay.' It was no coincidence that the journey started very early next morning and under cover of darkness.

It was the first of a number of stories about Mel's bad-boy behaviour to emerge from the making of *Summer City* that probably led to a more mature Gibson's rather sour, and perhaps unjustified, comments about the movie when challenged by journalists in later years.

The film itself was an uncomplicated story about four young men out for a good time against the bronzed and glamorous background of all-action surfing off those magnificent Australian beaches. Steve Bisley's Boo was the main character, an over-confident, self-opinionated brat, which he played with supreme arrogance. John Jarrat was equally convincing as a rather proper, controlled student with whom Bisley is almost constantly in conflict. Playing the role of mediators were Avalon himself, as Robbie, and Gibson as Scollop, the less intelligent, beach-bum surfer. The biggest joke during filming, and the most embarrassing moment for Mel, was when it was time to shoot the first scenes of him riding the heavy breakers. An astounded Avalon explained years later now in a calmer mood: 'The problem was that Mel simply could not ride a surfboard. The couple of times we sent him out to ride was a laugh.' In the end his surfing scenes were done by Ross Bailey, an expert surfer.

Billed variously as 'live fast, die young', a 'one-way trip back into the Sixties', 'funnier than *American Graffiti*, heavier than *Easy Rider*', *Summer City* was a typical low-budget picture which had taken its underlying message from a genre of moderately successful movies in America. It tracked four active males in vigorous, physical pursuit of a good-time weekend and, not altogether surprisingly perhaps when set against its restricted budget and the focus of the times, carried with standard-bearing flourish, all the enthusiastic Aussie stereotyping considered 'correct', popular and appropriate in the late 1970s. The plot comes with lots of action and characters are portrayed with vigour. Along with all the surfing, the picture includes a noisy local dance rave, the seduction of the land owner's virgin daughter, much drinking and quarrelling, a night out in the bush, and the climax of a fatal shoot-out. Avalon had the 26-year-old New Zealand-born Chris Fraser direct the picture which, later produced in 35mm form, was premiered in Sydney in December 1977.

Avalon came perilously close to running out of cash more than once and later admitted to being totally broke during the last week of shooting. He was reduced to borrowing from friends and had to cancel the standing arrangement he had made for the catering of cast and crew with a local shop. Gibson himself retains vivid memories of making his first picture and the rough-and-tumble nature of life on the set. Being in front of the movie cameras was a totally new experience for him and as a novice actor he wasn't expecting much in the way of luxury. Just as well. 'We wondered all the time whether we were going to eat, sleep, get paid or what,' he recalled. 'There was this madness as we went from day to day, a kind of excitement. It was a learning experience. We had to cope with bush fires. We slept on the floor of a local hall. But I would have done anything.'

Avalon agreed that the filming of *Summer City* was a highly informal affair. 'The accommodation was a hall with a couple of rooms off to one side,' he explained. 'Part of it was used as a production office, the rest absorbing props, wardrobe, make-up, equipment and all the other essential paraphernalia needed for movie-making.' The two rooms, situated on either side of the hall, were used by the cast and crew at night, males in sleeping bags down one side, females in sleeping bags down the other. Added comfort came courtesy of mattresses provided by Avalon. Gibson said that sleeping on the floor was no hardship and no one complained. 'Most of us crashed out early anyway, as we were shooting at dawn most days,' remembered Avalon.

Almost everyone involved with the making of *Summer City*

was on a learning curve, whether in front of the camera or not. Avalon himself was only twenty-eight and admitted he did not know much about making movies. 'But *Summer City* taught me a lot,' he said; and he would certainly go on to make bigger and more successful movies. Yet despite the film's precarious finances and the austere living conditions of the cast and crew, the making of *Summer City* was by no means dull and uneventful for the fun-loving twenty-year-old Gibson.

One reported occasion started innocently enough and ended in bedlam. Phil Avalon had agreed to give up, just for one night, the local hall he had hired as his production headquarters so that a wedding reception could be held there. An unexpected rumpus broke out, but Avalon wasn't unduly concerned. After all, he knew his crew would almost certainly be enjoying their time off in the local pubs, and were likely to stay there. But on arrival at the hall to investigate he was immediately besieged by angry wedding guests who lost no time in telling him what had happened. Two of his actors, it seems, had gate-crashed the reception, dropped their trousers and bared their backsides to the assembled guests, before promptly, laughingly, disappearing into the night. One backside, Avalon learned, was that of Steve Bisley, the other belonged to Mel Gibson.

Avalon later saw the funny side, but at the time admitted his difficulty in finding the right words with which to express his apology. Steve and Mel's courage had been bolstered by several beers, but Avalon said that the locals were so annoyed by the incident that it was more through guile and luck than approval that they found themselves back in the hall the next morning.

Mel and Steve's conduct, though unforgivable, was probably more stupid than intentionally arrogant or loutish. The story goes that at the time the habit of trouser-dropping was becoming something of an 'in' sport among the liveliest youngsters populating certain informal, uninhibited Pacific coastal areas of the United States. It was just unfortunate for Mel and Steve that the craze had not yet caught on in Australia. Certainly not in Catherine Hill Bay.

Of much more serious concern was the affair which Gibson had with actress Deborah Foreman, the female lead in *Summer City*. She was also twenty. Their relationship started after only a few days of shooting and developed rapidly. Deborah was infat-

43

uated, though by all accounts Gibson was not the all-consuming, always considerate, concerned escort. He was a very Australian man, she explained years later, no flowers or candlelit dinners. His matey friendships were important to him and Deborah admitted sometimes feeling a bit of an outcast when Mel and Steve Bisley got to fooling around. They continued to see one another after shooting on *Summer City* ended, but as Mel began to lose interest Deborah became increasingly possessive and distraught. In a moment of serious depression and anger, after Mel had broken away, she caused a sensation by cutting her wrists in a particularly upsetting incident at a 'drunken' party which they had both – though separately – attended. There was never a reconciliation and Deborah Foreman did not make another film.

Gibson's handsome looks and physical presence were by no means lost on the local girls or the female cast and crew members at Catherine Hill Bay. Those compelling blue eyes were an obvious turn-on and had been complemented by the need to have his shoulder-length hair severely cropped, and then dyed blond, for the picture. Australian actress Abigail, who also featured in *Summer City*, was struck by his looks, but even more so by his personality and presence. She recalled that he was quiet, even shy, though not transparent. 'There was something special there. You could see the makings of an actor,' she observed.

Years later Gibson would distance himself from *Summer City*, denouncing it as an abomination, a cheap and nasty flick. He would even attempt to gloss over it completely, suggesting in press interviews that his career had started with *Mad Max*. Not in doubt was the confidence and experience Gibson acquired from working on his first movie.

Avalon, in contrast, remembers the days they worked together at Catherine Hill Bay with much more affection. He has talked about Gibson's spirit of co-operation and helpfulness on the set, not just in acting through his scenes, but in his positive help in moving the film along generally by doing some of the chores around the place – useful, even essential, on a limited-budget picture. Avalon remembers that he would often volunteer. 'If there is anything I can do to help, just let me know,' he would say.

More positively, among those skilled and experienced enough to recognize the signs, Mel Gibson was quickly spotted as an actor of some promise. They could see his talent growing, day by day. Local girls and others arriving in the area on holiday would turn up during shooting and there was no shortage of moonstruck admirers. But he refused to be distracted. Even when not in a scene he would stay close to the action, learning and working things out in his own mind. That indefinable screen presence was there even then. More than once he impressed Chris Fraser. 'Give him more to do, more to say,' the director would suggest to Avalon. Always modest, where his own abilities were concerned, Gibson did not share Fraser's confidence.

When the cast and crew assembled for the first set of rushes and the first beach scene came up featuring Mel, he was critical, dissatisfied and almost embarrassed by what he saw of himself and the way he performed. But Fraser and Avalon independently formed a different view. They were so impressed that they wrote in a couple of extra scenes for him on the spot.

Because of its unambitious origins and generally low profile, *Summer City* was not fanfared on its release. Reviews were thin on the ground, and serious criticism was even more difficult to find. The Australian magazine *Cinema Papers* was almost out on its own in publishing a lengthy, well-studied assessment by Stephen Marston. He saw the theme of the picture as being distinctly 'Australian' at that time and 'an ideal subject for social and cultural comment, not to mention exploitation as film material.' On the credit side Marston approves the film's all-action plot, liking the way it 'rattles along very energetically and, at least, is never slow, boring or pretentious.' He singles out the sequence in which Boo (Bisley) seduces Caroline (Deborah Foreman) and her return home as 'moments of clarity, very sensitively photographed and acted,' but complains: 'We are allowed a very limited understanding of Boo and Sandy (John Jarrat); just Abigail, as a down-trodden pub wife, and Mel Gibson (Scollop) emerge as real people.'

Marston faults the way in which the film was directed, in what he called a scrappy and disjointed fashion, and disliked the way much of the dialogue is spoken off-camera. 'When the camera does move more closely,' he complains, 'the actors seem hampered by the simple-minded script, and their lines rush out quickly to make way for the action.'

Even so *Summer City* did reasonable business on release and

in the end made a small profit before gaining a kind of cult following when released on video. For a no-hoper picture put
together on a shoe-string budget, and which set out devoid of
commercial intent or ambition, that wasn't such a bad result
after all. Avalon, Fraser, Bisley, Gibson and the others ought not
to be too ashamed or embarrassed, whatever its shortcomings.

Summer City was also historic for another reason. Certainly
it gave Mel Gibson his start in pictures. Of course it unlocked
the door on his screen potential and his forthcoming enormous
sex appeal around the world. But also, of course, it was in
Summer City that Mel Gibson said his very first words in front
of the movie camera. Surely a historic moment. Picture the
scene. Mel, in short-sleeved red vest and blue jeans, knocks on
the car window where the Steve Bisley character is well into a
passionate kissing routine with a girl. Then Mel Gibson's character cuts in with this choice phrase spoken with a broad
Australian accent and a kind of leer. 'I thought you was going
bowling tonight.'

Memorable it might not have been, but the start of something
big for Gibson it certainly was. Who can say *Summer City* was
not important?

4   Just Call Me Mad Max

That Mel Gibson should find his way into some branch of the performing arts is not altogether surprising. Music was always important in the Gibson family home and the children grew to accept it as a natural part of everyday life. And in the shadows of recent history was the colourful example of Mel's paternal grandmother, Eva Mylott. It is easy to picture how the children would sit around in the evening, little eyes bright and wondrous, as they were told the captivating story of how she became a professional opera singer, helped and encouraged by none other than the world-famous Dame Nellie Melba; of how she sang to crowded concert halls in towns and cities in northern America and Canada; of her spirited personality and glamorous lifestyle; and how, in the Sydney Town Hall one day in February 1902, when she was twenty-seven, she gave her farewell performance before setting off for Europe with the echoes of repeated encores in her ears.

Mel's own father had a fine baritone voice, which was much admired by parishioners at St Patrick's Church in Verplanck and at numerous festivals and church concerts, while his 'feel for performance' was evident on those television quiz programmes on which he was so successful.

Still further evidence came from Mel's older sisters, Patricia and Sheila, both of whom sang professionally for a time. Patricia caught the performing bug early, appearing in school plays as both a junior and senior pupil and taking part in county festivals. Later she spent three years in London working professionally as a singer in a jazz band. Sheila, who initiated Mel's career by sending off that application form on his behalf to NIDA, had a musical career before her marriage, as a soloist on cruise ships sailing out of Sydney. Even closer to Mel in her ambition, sister Mary B studied drama after winning a scholarship at Syracuse University, but decided against acting professionally. Mel's youngest brother Donal, would follow Mel's example, studying at NIDA prior to becoming a professional actor and making some impact in the Australian film, *Fatal Bond*, produced, coincidentally, by Phil Avalon.

So if Gibson had followed some kind of family tradition by becoming a professional performer, the circumstances of his casting in the picture which rocket-launched him to instant stardom in Australia could not have been quirkier. For as with *Summer City*, he secured his role in *Mad Max* only after the first-choice actor pulled out. But this time Gibson was in the starring role.

Accounts of events at this time are often confusing and contradictory. According to Phil Avalon, it was he who rang casting agent Mitch Matthews to recommend she look at some footage from *Summer City*. 'I suggested Mel for a film that was to be made later that year called *Mad Max*,' he said. Others would claim it was Betty Williams, a voice teacher at NIDA, who set the ball rolling. But the major Gibson legend from this time concerned the pub brawl in which he was said to have been involved on 11 October 1977, on the eve of winning his role in *Mad Max*. According to reports, Mel was kicked and punched repeatedly, before collapsing to the floor. The police were called and someone telephoned for an ambulance. An eye-witness reported that Mel's eyes were already puffed and closing and his face was covered in blood. Gibson himself subsequently backed up the substance of this story more than once when talking to journalists. 'I was at a party and three guys really worked me over,' he explained some time later. 'Don't ask me why they came at me. I was an innocent party. I caught the worst of it. I had cuts and bruises and looked a mess.'

His face was still bruised and swollen, Mel claimed in subsequent interviews, when he attended a casting session for the new picture the following day. 'It was so bad I almost didn't turn up,' he said. Subsequent reports led to a widespread belief that his battered appearance even helped him secure the part, since he looked suitably rough and rugged, more like the character he would be playing. The story continued to gain ground despite

48

the comments of the casting director herself, Mitch Matthews. 'There is no way that Mel was in a fight,' she put on record. 'I have seen these stories and I know they are not true.' It is probably a question of timing, whether all this happened before or after he first went to see Mitch Matthews. It would certainly be before meeting director George Miller, who had the final word, and before starting work on the film. He was selected on merit, of that there is no doubt, and not because he looked battered. Miller said Mel was 'undamaged' when he cast him, but later saw a photograph of him 'after he had taken a beating.'

Never in dispute, however, was actor James Healy's appalling miscalculation and lost opportunity. Humping carcasses in a Melbourne abattoir at the time, the Irish-born Healy was desperate for a film role when he received the script to read. The part was virtually his for the taking, since director and co-writer George Miller had already stressed that they were looking for new faces, new talent for the picture. So there would be no competition from established stars. Healy eagerly read the script, but was desperately disappointed. In his view the picture had not the remotest chance of success and was stubbornly unimpressed when he saw that his potential character had only fourteen lines of dialogue in the whole filmscript. He brushed aside all attempts at persuasion and turned it down.

Meantime, Gibson's allotted spell at NIDA was coming to an end. It was September 1977 and he was on the verge of graduating. Healy was now out of the running and Miller was anxious to cast the lead role. He had already spent months trying to find an unknown who would be right in the part. 'In casting we didn't want anybody to be recognizable,' explained producer Byron Kennedy. 'We didn't want well-known faces taking attention from the stark reality of the action.' Casting director Mitch Matthews had already taken some video footage of Gibson and was impressed. 'He had such depth and sensitivity. He was pure magic,' she enthused.

Miller was shown the video and was equally convinced. Years later Gibson claimed that he just auditioned for a part in the picture. 'I didn't know I was going for the lead,' he said. 'I didn't really know what I was doing.' But such was Miller's determination to have Gibson in his picture that he decided to hold back the start of production until Gibson left NIDA on his graduation in October. It was a wise and significant move. The success of *Mad Max* would lead Miller into a couple of sequels, each picture becoming more successful than the one before, to bring him a level of recognition as a director much earlier than otherwise he could have expected, together with the personal credit for launching Mel Gibson on the road to international stardom.

George Miller, born in Brisbane in 1945, had early ambitions to become a doctor and graduated from the University of New South Wales medical school before going on to Melbourne University to study film and then to UCLA (University of California, Los Angeles), where he concentrated on acting. Miller continued to practise as a doctor while raising the money to finance *Mad Max*, which was his first feature film. Miller himself saw nothing deeply significant about it; no hidden messages. One reference work lists it simply as 'a low-budget, biker-exploitation movie set in an arid, post-industrial wasteland.'

Mad Max was the joint creation of Miller and Byron Kennedy, and both worked with co-writer James McCausland on the script. Miller had met Kennedy while working at a hospital in Sydney, but his obsession with film-making had taken root years before, when he was a youngster in his home village in Queensland, where he never tired of visiting his local picture house for Saturday matinees. It was when Miller attended a series of lectures given by Byron Kennedy at a film school in Melbourne that they became friends. Miller later gave up being a medic to write scripts for low-budget and experimental films produced by Kennedy, learning his skills the hard way as sound man, camera man and editor for documentary films and in television.

By 1977 Miller's thoughts about a genre movie had begun to crystallize. Through his work with McCausland, a screenplay emerged that was sufficiently different in concept, dialogue and vision to be almost revolutionary. For who would want to see a picture about the aftermath of a monstrous event which devastated the landscape, featured unknown actors and with a rag-tag hero less than six feet tall who had only fourteen lines of dialogue in the entire film? And all this almost a decade before the comic-book heroics of Stallone and Schwarzenegger!

Cutting down the dialogue was an intentional ploy and recognized Miller's enormous admiration for the old silent films, which had to rely on action, gesture and innuendo to convey the messages. *Mad Max* was to be a film of action. So why not follow the example of those silent stars of yesteryear, Harold Lloyd and Buster Keaton? 'They really understood that images were film language; that a film is sound and pictures, not talking and pictures,' said Miller. But in advance of filming, and even after the picture had been shot, *Mad Max* offered little hope of success. For Gibson though, success was not all that important. What really mattered was that he had secured his first part in a 'proper' commercial film and, moreover, had been cast in the lead role, straight out of drama school. What more could he want?

The film was a monumental risk for Miller, but one he was prepared to take if he could keep the budget down. He explained that his first idea was simply to make a low-budget genre film, something like a car exploitation movie. The cops, baddies and a revenge story developed out of that. More precisely, the unusual profile of the picture, with its absence of major stars demanding huge payments (only Australian Roger Ward was known, and then only in his own country), and no elaborate sets to construct, was one way of hacking down costs to a manageable size. More than half the cast and crew had never worked on a feature film before.

Against this background it is astonishing that Miller was able to turn in a film which was not only considered a worthy piece of entertainment that struck gold but also became widely regarded as setting new standards in Australian film production. That was a notable achievement when considered against the dark and cynical overtones of *Mad Max*, for it is about anarchy and disorder, black leather-clad policemen in rocket-like cars, a pitched battle between Max and murderous thugs, a massacre and a horde of motorcyclists. It had been a long, hard road for Miller and Kennedy as they battled to raise money. In the end it was considered a minor miracle that such an extravagant-looking, all-action, great-outdoors movie like *Mad Max* could be made without considerable outside finance.

The picture was tough, brutal, ruthless and spectacular. Gibson was given a glimpse of just how rugged it would be when he first visited Miller at his rambling old house in the Melbourne suburbs. A heavily bandaged man opened the door and Gibson

51

thought he must be at the wrong house. But he wasn't. The man who had welcomed him inside was Grant Page, the picture's stunt man. Though the picture was not yet shooting, Gibson quickly realized that rehearsing the spectacular stunts for which the picture would become famous was already claiming victims. It was Miller's house, incidentally, which would become home for cast and crew during the time the picture was being made. It was generally a crowded scene there with beds and mattresses littered about most rooms. The scenes were shot not too far away, mainly at a desolate area just outside Melbourne.

The film was promoted as a Gothic horror story set in the near future. 'The location is Australia . . . a few years from now. Urban society is in terminal decay. The intercity highways have become white line nightmares; the arena for a strange, apocalyptic death game between nomad bikers and a handful of young cops in souped-up pursuit cars.'

Gibson plays Max Rockatansky, a young cop responsible for the death of a crazed biker known as the Nightrider, played by Vince Gill. Max is facing a crossroads in life. His woman Jessie (Joanne Samuel) wants him to quit the road. Fifi Macaffee (Roger Ward), the bald-headed boss of the road cops, wants to keep him in the force and has commissioned a supercharged pursuit special as an inducement. When a gang of nomad bikers led by a charismatic psychopath known as the Toecutter (Hugh Keays-Byrne) ride into a small railway town to collect the remains of the Nightrider, they come into violent conflict with the local townspeople and respond by chasing a young couple out into the countryside and literally tear apart their hot-rod. Max and his cop colleague and buddy, the Goose, played by his close friend and co-star from *Summer City*, Steve Bisley, come across the aftermath of this vandalism where they find a drug-crazed Johnny the Boy left behind by the bikers.

When next day Johnny is released from custody by the ineffectual court system, the frustrated head of police, Fifi, gives his boys an open ticket to do whatever they feel is necessary on the roads. Open warfare breaks out. The Goose, marked for revenge by the nomad bikers, survives a monumental prang after his motorcycle is tampered with, but dies a few hours later after gang members get to him. Max visits his friend in hospital and is horrified to witness the last moments of his life. Max quits the force and takes his wife Jessie and their young child, Sprog, across the Australian landscape in their van, the sad memories and dark fears all but forgotten.

But there is more pursuit, violence and anguish. Max and Jessie are hunted by the bikers in a series of suspense sequences. Jessie sustains fearful injuries and Sprog dies. As Jessie fights for survival in hospital, Max changes. Revenge takes over and he becomes *Mad Max*. He returns to the police force and sets up the pursuit special. One by one he hunts down the nomad bikers before driving on and away into the wastelands – a link to a potential sequel (*Mad Max 2: The Road Warrior*). Interestingly, Jessie's death from her injuries is not confirmed by the first film, though perhaps implied. Miller and Kennedy agreed as much in later times and there was even said to be a brief shot of a grave at the start of the uncut version of *Mad Max 2*. Max's revenge is all the deeper because he hears of his wife's terrible injuries and knows she cannot recover. Her immediate death on the road, with the child, would have eliminated any hope of her survival from the outset and in the end would perhaps not have hurt him so much.

This high-pressure melting-pot of law and order in serious decline was a tough assignment for a 21-year-old actor whose foot was hardly on the bottom rung of the ladder. The schedule called for a gruelling eighteen-hour day and the shoot lasted three weeks. Between takes Mel would sit quietly, absorbing the detail and atmosphere. One of the cast remembered: 'He didn't act like the star of the movie at all. He didn't say much, but was always ready and well prepared when it was time for him to go in front of the cameras.' It might have been easier if there had been more lines for him to say. His quiet composure was something of a talking point and was first noticed at a pre-filming party which Miller had given at his home. Gibson just hung about for a time, saying little and barely mixing, and then apparently disappeared early to learn his lines.

Mad Max was not everyone's cup of tea. But, as one report pointedly explained, 'with a higher thrill-per-frame rate than almost any other thriller before or since, rock-video directors would spend ten years imitating the *Max* style.' Making a movie out of such a lurid, distasteful theme led to accusations from many quarters of naked exploitation, pandering to baser instincts for purely commercial reasons. More serious perhaps were the genuine fears in some quarters that it might glamorize violence.

Gibson's attitude was predictable, though perhaps slightly contradictory. He hinted at fears that bikers might just take it a little too seriously. This came after he unknowingly followed the example of film star Fred Astaire almost fifty years earlier, when the dance legend self-consciously sneaked unrecognized into a small, neighbourhood cinema in Augusta, Maine, to see a public showing of his first film. But when Gibson slipped into a Sydney cinema to see himself as *Mad Max* as others would see him, he found he was among an audience of bikers. Nobody noticed him, but at the end he admitted he was a little worried by their reaction. 'A lot of them seemed to take it a little too seriously,' he observed. At another time he expressed no concern at all. 'It's a cartoon . . . you have to remember that,' he explained casually. Others would set it up as simply a new-genre western, the cowboys and Indians, the goodies and the baddies, but in a different setting. Even Miller's ambitions were hardly more lofty: 'I set out to create a futuristic western,' he said.

The film scored heavily for its startling and impressive stunt sequences. Fourteen stuntmen and precision drivers carried out all the fast-moving action. Many of the chase and action sequences were filmed at speeds of up to 145 m.p.h. (240 k.p.h.). A specially prepared vehicle was used to capture the high-speed shots and to protect both the camera, mounted on the vehicle, and the crew travelling at speed.

Some scenes were so realistic and fast-moving that unofficial records were set. Nothing before on film had come close to their intensity. Two particular stunts were breathtaking. In the first, bikes and riders surge out of control at maximum revs, careering off a bridge and falling into the river below, the low camera angle emphasizing the pace and tension of the sequence. The other is a head-on collision between a 1000cc Kawasaki motorcycle and a 12-cylinder Kenworth truck. Rapid camera flashes from one to the other lead to graphic realism as the bike and rider are sucked underneath the braking truck. A world first was the use of a solid-fuel rocket motor to propel a vehicle to 100 m.p.h. (160 k.p.h.) over a distance of just 30 metres. It took three whole days to shoot this critical four seconds of finished film, and so intricate were the technical aspects involved that the stunt was filmed after the main body of shooting was over.

Grant Page's nine-man stunt team, each man chosen carefully for his special skills, captured attention for their daring and remarkable technique. Page's daunting task, assisted by racing-driver Phil Brock and French driver George Novak, was the coordination of 114 separate stunt scenes. Gerry Gauslaa, one of Australia's top motorcycle riders, jumped a big, 4-cylinder motorcycle 76 feet (24 metres) before separating from the bike in mid-flight. The task for Dale Bensch and Michael Daniells was straightforward and well defined: to dismount from their motorcycles while travelling at 55 m.p.h. (90 k.p.h.) and allowing their machines to crash and tumble over their sparsely protected bodies. Grant Page put himself in the driving seat of a Ford Falcon which crashed through a caravan at 80 m.p.h. (130 k.p.h.) and charged an undefended van at 85 m.p.h. (140 k.p.h.).

Miller was still largely inexperienced and had to change, adjust, delete and create as he went along. This didn't make life any easier for the actors, Mel included. And astonishingly, all filming took place on main roads and highways around Melbourne. Very rigid safety procedures were put in place to protect the cast, crew and the public and to supervise the total clearance of sections of road and highway. Ian Goddard, a former winner of the 24-hour Le Mans motorcycle grand prix, was in charge of safety. It is much to his credit, and his team of four assistants who supervised traffic through an extensive radio communications link-up, that not a single accident occurred during filming. Ironically, journeys to and from the location proved to be less safe. After only four days of shooting Grant Page and leading lady Rosie Bailey were involved in a motor accident. Both sustained broken legs, Page also suffering a broken nose and kidney damage. But while he was able to continue, temporarily slipping out of his bandages and splints to do a stunt, Bailey lost her lead role because of the accident and was replaced by Joanne Samuel. Fourteen vehicles were written off during filming and five V8 motors and five gearboxes blew up. A team of three mechanics worked round the clock to keep the production on the road.

While Australian film director Peter Weir is seen as a key player in the renaissance of Australian film in the late 1970s, there is little doubt that George Miller made his contribution with *Mad Max*. His film was entertaining, simple in concept and approach, and influential. Its success in Australia particularly and then in other parts of the world including the United States, proved it had captured the mood of the times, especially among younger audiences. The film won six Australian Film Institute awards and Mel, despite the crippling handicap of those meagre fourteen lines of dialogue, captured the best actor award. The picture broke attendance records in Japan and when it moved strongly on to the American market, despite the savage response of the American critics, it secured the kind of wide distribution previously unheard-of for an Australian contemporary film. In the United States Mel's dialogue was dubbed because distributors felt home audiences would struggle with his Australian accent. It would also make a strong impact as a cult movie in the UK and in many other countries.

George Miller later tried to explain its success. 'It somehow managed to transcend many cultural boundaries,' he said. Miller's adoption of the basic theme of hero versus villains meant that it could be as easily absorbed in Japan as in Europe or America. The lone figure in black leather pitted against the world, the saviour of mankind, was the oldest story in the book, but as *Mad Max* proved, still one of the very best. Black leather achieved cult fashion status, even among women. Gibson's instant conversion into a cinematic heart-throb is largely down to the way Miller presented him to the public, according to writer David Ragan. Another astute assessment came from Canadian writer Terry Poulton.

In *Mad Max* the camera repeatedly focuses on his black leather boots and then pans slowly, tantalizingly upward. If that sounds like the treatment usually given only to female movie stars, it is. But the only thing remotely feminine about Gibson is the vulnerability he projects ... Audiences sense that there is an unusual set of elements in this particular psyche, and they are right.

The making of *Mad Max* was a gruelling experience. Miller confessed it was a nightmare to shoot. That automobile accident before shooting began, which meant replacing the female lead, lost him two weeks of critical production time. The whole of the early part of the film had to be rescheduled. 'Most nights I was up until 1 a.m. working out what we could shoot the next day,' Miller explained. Though physically and mentally drained by the end, Miller was amply compensated by the huge success of the film.

His choice of Gibson for the starring role was fully vindicated. The future star had no pedigree to speak of, was theoretically, in height and bulk, not altogether the physical ideal, but he fully repaid Miller's confidence in him. What Gibson showed in his first major movie was the onset of that intangible, yet powerful physical presence on the screen. Even against the grey, barren landscape of the film his dark sexual presence shone through. Some critics would go so far as to say that without Gibson's charismatic presence *Mad Max* could well have been a very ordinary film, a possible failure even.

Gibson himself appeared rather unimpressed, claiming that the picture was quite uneven, and muddled – no one knew quite what to make of it. This was arrogant enough judgement from someone not long out of drama school with one minor picture to his credit, though perhaps not too wide of the mark. Miller, too, openly acknowledged its flaws. More to the point, however, was his shrewd identification of the changing need of a cinema-going public becoming bored by artistically valid, but downbeat fare. The somewhat gloomy portrayals of life in Australia, then in vogue, were never likely to make an impression on big screens around the globe – especially not in the massive North American market. But it was another matter whether the electrifying pace, grey images, gaunt landscapes and sheer physical vigour of his new film was too radical a step for audiences to take in one gulp. Certainly, no one involved with the picture was sufficiently confident to hang around long enough to find out. Livings had to be earned.

With *Mad Max* behind him and his days at NIDA over, Gibson settled down to extend his experience on the stage. He joined the State Theatre Company of South Australia in Adelaide. At this point he still had no thoughts of turning film-making into a life-long career; did not even know, after just two movies, whether it was even an option. In any event, he preferred stage work and was still a relatively unknown actor trying to make a name for himself in secondary roles in such plays as *Oedipus Rex, Henry IV* and *Cedona*.

First hints that *Mad Max* might be something more than just another picture in Gibson's early career came from his agents more than 1,000 miles away in Sydney. The picture had yet to be released when Faith Martin and Bill Shanahan picked up those early, significant signals. George Miller was trumpeting Gibson's performance for all he was worth and Michael Pate, an Australian-born former Hollywood actor, was keen to know. He was slated to direct a new picture based on the Colleen McCullough novel *Tim* and contacted Martin and Shanahan to see if Gibson might be interested and available.

They promptly sent him a copy of the early screen test which Mel had made. Pate was impressed and arrangements were made for the two men to meet. Gibson at twenty-two years old was still undisciplined, disorganized and a tatty dresser. Pate was unimpressed. He had seen Gibson in *Summer City*, but had not recognized him because of his dyed blond hair. When their meeting continued in a hotel over a couple of drinks, Gibson made a firmer impression. Pate decided to take a chance and offered him the part.

For the third time running, Gibson would be stepping into someone else's shoes. Pate had been on the point of confirming his own son Christopher in the leading role when Gibson stepped into the picture.

5 On the Way to Gallipoli

The success of *Mad Max* was still under the surface when Gibson began shooting his new film under the direction of Michael Pate. It would still be some time before the picture was released. His bank balance, if not a cause for despair, was not exactly inspiring either. Just as well that future security and an expensive lifestyle were not his top priorities. After all, he was still in his early twenties – single, carefree and indifferent to the high life. He spent little on clothes and was happy enough with cash in his pocket to buy beers and cigarettes.

Despite the carefree existence, he was strongly focused in front of the camera. Although word had not reached him yet, he was quietly becoming known in the business. So he was happy enough when not one, but two pictures were lined up for him within just a few months. In addition, a much more significant development was looming, the chance to star in a major new movie, *Gallipoli*. When the time came, he would seize the opportunity to show his serious potential as a film actor of substance.

Meanwhile he was content to leave South Australia and his stage career behind to return to familiar Sydney territory, joining Michael Pate on the set of his new film, *Tim*. Pate, born in Australia, had courageously moved to Hollywood almost thirty years before, where he made successful appearances in dozens of movies while learning just about all there was to know about movie-making. He returned to Australia to go into film production and wrote the screenplay of *Tim*, based on Colleen McCullough's book of the same name; and he also planned to direct the picture.

Tim was a sensitive tale light years away from the thundering energy and pace of *Mad Max*, but Gibson was happy to cross the bridge for the sake of his art. At this point the most obviously exciting aspect of the project was that Hollywood star Piper Laurie, whose first substantial screen role in *The Hustler* in 1961 had earned her an Oscar nomination, had agreed to take the female lead opposite Gibson.

The six-week shoot took place in an area of outstanding beauty, around the northern peninsula of Sydney, and much of the picture would be filmed at Palm Beach, New South Wales, in the home of former film and stage celebrities Googie Withers and John McCallum. It was again a tough test for the relatively inexperienced Gibson. He admitted he was nervous. 'I'd never really received direction before,' he claimed, adding that in his two earlier pictures he had simply gone on set and played the part as best he could. Pate was quick to spot that his new star really had very little film technique. 'But he learned quickly and he learned well,' he said. Gibson had to try and hold his own among all the competent and expert people around him. 'We'd all been in the business for some time and were very experienced,' acknowledged Pate. Gibson was a raw novice by comparison. Yet even then he made an impact as an instinctive professional. He had studied his role and scenes so thoroughly that he quickly became known as 'one-take Mel'.

It was not an easy part, even for an actor of experience. After only a couple of low-budget pictures, and all the high-tension drama and physical excitement of *Mad Max*, Gibson's role as the moderately mentally retarded Tim, a young man who develops a fond relationship with an attractive woman almost twice his age, was a test of his acting range, calling for the most tender and sensitive portrayal. Admittedly he had more than fourteen lines of dialogue to help him. He and co-star Piper Laurie between them carry most of the film and are responsible for the gentle progression of the plot. The challenge for both of them was to make this simple story credible, meaningful and, at times, emotionally intense.

Mel, as Tim Melville, is a good-looking, pleasant young man of twenty-five, who is doing casual work around the house of neighbour Mary Horton (Laurie), an attractive, unmarried woman in her mid forties. When Mary's gardener leaves her employ because of an injured back, the gentle, tender and co-operative Tim takes over on a regular basis. Their mutual courtesy grows slowly into friendship. Tim likes the way Mary treats him, sympathetically but as a normal, mentally healthy person. For her part, Mary enjoys helping Tim develop his restricted intellect and expand his interests into new areas like painting.

Tim is distraught when his sister marries. He cannot really understand what marriage is, until Mary explains. He is further traumatized when his mother becomes ill and dies. Mary seeks the guidance and advice of professionals to see how she can help Tim. In doing so she finds herself benefiting from the contact and gaining a more profound inner contentment. But what is really happening is that Mary is growing closer to Tim. It takes her employer to make her realize that she has fallen in love with Tim, and he indeed with her, and that they should marry, on the basis that most of their obvious doubts and problems can be solved.

Gibson and Laurie worked well together, got on well together. He was not intimidated by the vast experience and Hollywood reputation of his co-star. She admired his portrayal. 'It's not an easy role, yet he brings a warmth and presence to Tim you expect only from an actor who has been around for a long time,' she said, as the picture neared completion. Pate also admired Gibson's work, mentioning qualities like pathos, taste and humour. He said that Gibson brought a great depth to what was a highly instinctive performance.

Even this early in his career Gibson seldom talked about all the work he did to prepare himself for a role. It was out of tune with the casual, dashing lifestyle he liked to convey, and indeed enjoy, when not filming. He habitually worked harder than his breezy personality suggested.

Those who knew him well enough were not surprised when, as the picture was about to start shooting, he said he could not really give a contact address, as is normal in the business, since he was not altogether clear where he would be staying while the film was being made. Pate had little choice but to accept the inevitable, but going through his mind was, What do I do if we are all set to shoot one morning with the dollars ticking away and there is no sign of our male lead? It never happened. Mel provided a number of different accommodation addresses and, according to technicians on the set, seemed to arrive for work from a different direction every morning. But he always showed up, and there were no emotional outbursts or prima donna tantrums.

Surprising, for the majority who knew him less well, was Gibson's preparation for the role and his delicate, precise assessment of how he should play the character. A fine line had to be drawn and Gibson admitted it was a challenge. 'It wasn't a question of playing someone retarded, a love-smitten, illiterate young man, but rather stressing the innocence aspect of it, as if he were someone normal with a link missing somewhere, but offering love and loyalty without guile,' he explained with typical candor. He said he had read the book and knew how he was going to play Tim, pointing out that he had also studied the behaviour of his seven-year-old nephew and made some visits to mental institutions. Not that his nephew was retarded, but it gave him a link to innocence, instincts and the simplicity of life. 'I couldn't have played him drooling – it would have been a turn-off,' he added.

On release *Tim* did reasonable business in Australia, but made little impact on the outside world with only a limited showing in America. Critics were largely unmoved by it, though Gibson's performance was rated highly in many quarters and would earn him the Australian Film Institute Best Actor Award.

Gibson would remember *Tim* as a happy experience. Piper Laurie praised both Michael Pate and Mel Gibson – Pate for recognizing the potential in Gibson and then for taking a chance and casting him in the role. Gibson because, as she explained, 'Mel *was* Tim . . . sheer magic.' She said he was fun to work with and when she went home she told everybody about 'this wonderful young actor in Australia'. Mel's performance was also admired by author Colleen McCullough. 'Mel was absolutely right for the part,' she declared. This was in strong contrast with the time her more famous book, *The Thorn Birds*, was made into a TV mini-series starring Richard Chamberlain, when she felt disillusioned and let-down. With *Tim* she felt that justice had been done to the book she had written.

His current film-making over, Gibson returned to Sydney for a stint at the Nimrod Theatre, which was a venue for NIDA graduates to gain experience in their chosen profession, though sadly it went bankrupt in 1987 and the premises were threatened with takeover by the Sydney City Council. A rescue attempt resulted in the formation of the Belvoir Street Theatre, with some $500,000 having been raised on appeal to former NIDA graduates and supporters, including Mel Gibson and Judy Davis, who contributed $1,000 each. As recently as early 1998 when this book was going to press the Belvoir Street Theatre was still in operation; and according to sources there Gibson still holds the original share.

Back in the late 1970s Gibson reprised his early NIDA lead role in *Romeo and Juliet* at the Nimrod and immediately followed this up with *No Names, No Pack Drill*, in which he played an absconding US Marine in Sydney in 1942 who has an affair with an Australian nightclub singer. He went on to receive rave notices in the Samuel Beckett play, *Waiting for Godot*, in which he had appeared a few years earlier. These stage appearances called for a keen understanding of, and total conviction to, widely differing roles. His part in the Beckett play was especially tough, sapping his energy and considerably reducing his body weight. The critics were impressed with his performance and the public appetite for the young Mel Gibson surged after the release of *Mad Max*. His agents were swamped with requests about his availability.

If Gibson had accelerated his career with *Tim*, his next movie can only be viewed as a backward step. Later he would be so disgusted with himself for signing to do *Attack Force Z* that he simply refused to talk about it. The bitterness of his response, when he was reluctantly drawn to comment, was barely repeatable: 'A piece of shit,' was one of his kindlier spontaneous remarks. Struggling to find a grain of consolation he lamely suggested that one can learn something from doing almost anything. What he learned from *Attack Force Z* was simple: never do anything like it again.

So what went wrong? After all, the story, if not the most inspiring of all time, was neither the most banal. Billed as an adventure drama, the picture follows an Australian squad of special Z Force soldiers during World War Two being taken from Australia by submarine to infiltrate a Japanese-occupied island in the Pacific. Their task is to locate a VIP reportedly lost during an air crash, or to check for certain that he is dead. The cast, with

Gibson supposedly in the lead role of Captain Paul Kelly, included several other significant players. There was the Northern Ireland-born character actor Sam Neill, who had already caught the eye of international audiences in Gillian Armstrong's *My Brilliant Career*, John Phillip Law, who had starred alongside Jane Fonda in *Barbarella* and notable Australian actors John Waters and Chris Haywood.

A surprise switch of director might have signalled problems, but should not have done so since Philip Noyce, originally down to direct, and Tim Burstall, who took over when Noyce left even before shooting began, both had good track records in the business. The cast and crew were full of confidence when they took off for Taiwan to make the film. But the six-week shoot was marred by clashes over script changes and disputes over pay differentials among the leading players, souring relationships. This led to arguments over who was in the main role and allegations that John Phillip Law was being paid considerably more than Gibson and Neill simply because of his influence in attracting the finance crucial to the picture.

It did not help that *Attack Force Z* was a co-production. Such ventures often run into trouble because of disputes over approach and emphasis – a grudging compromise, however unpalatable, has to be found if the picture is to go forward. Almost half the actors and technicians were Chinese. They would stop work suddenly for no good reason and start again only on the promise of extra pay being handed over.

All this contributed to Gibson's condemnation of the final product. He probably felt his $A6,000 fee did not compensate for the aggravation of the filming, particularly since he claimed that he had done the picture only for the money. He would later bitterly attack the picture 'as a vulgar attempt at a war-action movie'. Nor did it help that the release of the film was delayed. But although it was consigned to perdition by Gibson and others personally involved in the shambles of its making, not all critics considered it to be that bad. The American magazine, *Variety*, felt it to be a 'good example of a well-paced, finely acted war film'. More investment, more stability and a stronger individual focus from just one production company might have helped its chances of healthier box-office receipts. As it was, *Attack Force Z* never made it on general release to American cinemas, though it did show up on cable TV and became available on video.

Meanwhile, far away from Taiwan, the pieces were falling into place for what would prove a much happier and more profitable experience for Gibson. The key player in the germinating scenario was Australian film director Peter Weir, whose career had started modestly with a fifteen-minute black-and-white 16 mm film released in 1967 when he was only twenty-three. Two years later he won a Young Film-makers Award in Australia and in 1970 co-wrote and directed *Michael*, though his writing contribution was relatively minor. The picture was part of a Commonwealth Film Unit trilogy on youth and it won the Grand Prix at the Australian Film Awards of 1970. *Homesdale*, a fifty-minute 16 mm feature, won him the same award the following year and in 1974 his picture, *The Cars that Ate Paris*, became a cult film that was screened around the world. In 1975 Peter Weir directed *Picnic at Hanging Rock*, which was written by Cliff Green from the Joan Lindsay novel and had Patricia Lovell as executive producer. Not only was the film a breakthrough for Weir, it came to represent the resurgence of Australian cinema.

It was in 1976, when Weir was on his way to London for the opening of this picture, that he made a detour to visit Gallipoli. He had been thinking for some time about making a World War One film with the story set in France and dealing with the big battles of Verdun, the Somme and Ypres on the Western Front in 1916–17. 'Then someone said to me, why not make a film about Gallipoli, it's the obvious one,' he explained afterwards.

After hiring a car in Istanbul, Weir drove to the battlefield and almost immediately his mind was made up. 'It was an extraordinary experience,' he remembered. 'I saw no one in two days of climbing up and down the slopes and wandering through the trenches, finding all sorts of scraps left by the armies – buttons and bits of old leather, belts, bones of donkeys. I felt I was really touching history and it totally altered my perception of Gallipoli. I decided then and there that I'd make the film.'

Weir began his research by reading the official history by C.E.W Bean and *The Broken Years* by Bill Gammage, an anthology of excerpts from soldiers' diaries and letters. He wrote the first draft himself before handing over to screenwriter David

Williamson, a playwright who had helped to revive the Australian theatre. His play, *The Club*, played the Lyceum on Broadway in 1978 and in Australia it grossed over a million dollars at the box office. Film rights were later sold for a record fee for Australia. Weir's script for *Gallipoli* was the first of a series of drafts which would lead to a change in his original thoughts on how the picture should be angled. Weir explained:

> At first we thought we would tell the whole story from enlistment in 1914 through to the evacuation of Gallipoli at the end of 1915, but we were not getting at the burning centre that had made Gallipoli a legend. So we put the legend to one side and simply made up a story about two young men, really got to know them, where they came from, what happened to them along the way, spent more time getting to the battle and less time on the battlefield.

Gallipoli, therefore, became a fictional account of two young men on the road to adventure, how they crossed the deserts of the outback, continents and great oceans, climbed the pyramids and walked through the ancient sands of Egypt to make their appointment with destiny in the real historical débâcle at Gallipoli.

When the time came to cast the picture Weir remembered Gibson, whose performance in *Mad Max* had greatly impressed him. Producer Patricia Lovell had also, independently, added a tick alongside Gibson's name. Indeed, had it not been for Pat Lovell, Gibson might have slipped through the casting net for *Gallipoli*. Mel had heard that Peter Weir wanted to do a picture as long as three years before it became a reality. At that time he was testing for a part in another Patricia Lovell film, when she asked him to take a look at the first draft of *Gallipoli*, pointing out the role of Frank. The upshot was that Gibson auditioned and director Peter Weir hired him on the spot. Mel met screenwriter David Williamson the very next day and started his indepth research straight away.

Gibson would later explain that Weir cast him as Frank Dunne because of a certain hard-edged quality, which was right for the part. Mel assessed his own role like this: 'Frank is a strange bag of tricks. More complicated than the average young man at that time . . . his survival instinct was really strong.' He added that Frank was not a hero, but showed flashes of bravery when cornered.

When Weir approached agents Bill Shanahan and Faith Martin to check Gibson's availability the timing was perfect. Mel had been bombing around Sydney to little purpose since finishing the ill-fated *Attack Force Z*. The one occasion that lifted his spirits was when he and the 24-year-old Robyn Denise Moore got married. He had reluctantly taken a part in a television drama, *Punishment*, but his heart was never in it. His income was meagre and his career seemed to have stalled. So he was more than delighted when told about the opportunity to star in *Gallipoli*.

The name evokes huge emotions in Australia because of the slaughter of Australian and New Zealand troops in an ill-fated campaign that was eventually abandoned on 20 December 1915 after ten months of bad luck, muddle, indecisiveness – and outstanding heroism. The sorry story of the Gallipoli campaign began as a confident attempt to knock Turkey, Germany's ally, out of the war, but by the time the combined land and sea operation was mounted at the end of April 1915, a full two months after the Navy had first bombarded the Dardanelles forts, all advantages of surprise had been lost and the Turks had heavily reinforced their positions.

A unique first-hand perspective of events was conveyed by Jack Gearing, the last survivor of the naval operations off the Gallipoli peninsula, shortly before his death aged 102 in early 1997. 'Each day when there was a lull we'd go in and collect the wounded; some of them were terribly badly wounded and all so young,' explained Mr Gearing, who had served on the cruiser *Theseus* when she landed British troops at Suvla Bay at the start of the campaign in August and again in the two evacuations of troops in December 1915 and January 1916. 'We weren't succeeding at all,' remembered Mr Gearing of those distant events. 'All we were doing was losing a lot of men and ships. Every day we were bringing in different men, different faces, all tired, all beaten.'

The two evacuations, over a period of eleven nights, were about the only successes of the whole campaign. More than 120,000 men with their guns, vehicles, horses and equipment were spirited away by night with only a handful of injuries and without the loss of a single life.

For Britain, Gallipoli was but one disaster in a long-suffering, fearsome and bloody war. For the new nation of Australia Gallipoli became a legend. To appreciate its significance to Australians it is important to go back to 1914, when World War One began. Australia, though a member of the British Commonwealth, seemed detached and geographically remote, and yet the country wanted to stand alongside Britain. Australians who enlisted were not professional soldiers. Bushmen rode hundreds of miles to their nearest city to enlist and there joined many others from all walks of life who went to war with the true spirit of adventure. It was an adventure that turned into a gruesome nightmare.

Britain had sent out crack troops to capture the tactically important Dardanelles Straits. When the British attack bogged down, the Australian and New Zealand troops were sent in as a diversion in what turned out to be an ill-planned and bloody assault. To begin with, the troops were landed at the wrong cove many miles from their target. The operation, meant to surprise the Turks, was met by a barrage of fire from the waiting troops. Of the 20,000 Australian and New Zealand troops landed, there were more than 8,000 casualties in the first twenty-four hours. But they dug in and maintained their foothold on Anzac Cove until being evacuated. Ever since, antipodeans have celebrated 25 April as Anzac Day, the day the Australian and New Zealand Army Corps (Anzac) landed at Gallipoli.

The story of Gallipoli resonates with a massive emotional power, as Peter Weir discovered when the idea began to consume him. The Australian director would have known about two previous film accounts. *Tell England* (1931) had dealt cursorily with the Dardanelles campaign; *40,000 Horsemen* (1940) was a tribute to the Australian Light Horse. But he knew that if his own vision was to succeed in the 1980s, it would have to set aside the gung-ho flag-waving spirit in favour of conviction, realism, objectivity – and convey a sense of deep commitment.

Having chosen to personalize the story through the decisions, lives and emotions of its two main characters, Weir realized that judicious casting was vital. Newcomer Mark Lee was chosen to play Archy Hamilton alongside Gibson's key role as Frank Dunne, a likeable rogue innocently caught up in the ravages of war.

Gibson had not thought too much about Gallipoli and the Anzac campaign since studying textbooks and maps at school, but was soon reading anything he could find on the subject. Typically thorough in his preparations, he read the official accounts and talked to people who had a close knowledge. He picked through letters and diaries. Simply getting to know in some detail what happened was not enough. He researched the background and origins of the war itself and the events which led to Gallipoli. He needed to discover the extreme emotions of his character, who would find the shocking reality of war far from the glory and heroism he imagined. 'I grew very close to my character and felt there was a lot of Frank in me and vice versa,' Gibson explained. He considered it his favourite role up to that time. The film was also widely considered to be one of the most impressive ever to come from Australia.

Mark Lee (Archy) plays an eighteen-year-old farmboy and champion sprinter who is trained by a fiercely demanding, though well-intentioned uncle (Bill Kerr). It is 1915 and Archy wants to do his bit for wartime Australia. After winning the coveted trophy at the Fremantle athletics meeting, he tells his uncle that he intends to enlist. Everyone else is joining up. It is what young men were doing. Running him close in the race was Frank Dunne (Gibson), a railway worker and a native of Perth. Despite their keen rivalry in the running competition the two boys become firm friends. Before shooting began, both men had to toughen up for the sprint sequences. A slimline Mark Lee added required muscle through weight-training in the gym, while Gibson found his cigarette smoking left him short of puff when put to the test. Vigorous exercises trimmed his physique and improved his lung capacity.

Tempted by Archy's idea of going into the army, Frank decides to join his new-found friend and they enlist together, though much to their dismay they are appointed to different regiments. They find themselves reunited at a training camp in Egypt and are able to stay together after Archy talks his commanding officer into allowing Frank to transfer into the Light Horse Regiment. They enjoy a boisterous friendship on their way to Gallipoli.

Under fire in the trenches, Archy (Lee) is given hope of survival when appointed runner to the officer-in-charge, relaying vital communications from the British trenches. He acts with supreme courage when, seeing how terrified Frank (Gibson) has become as the next onslaught approaches, he generously exchanges places. The odds are so overwhelmingly in favour of the Turks that the next time-scheduled order to advance surely must be withdrawn. The Anzacs wait in hope for the arrival of Frank which will spare the men the machine guns' slaughter.

At last Frank receives the order from the officer-in-charge and races desperately for his home trench with the vital message of reprieve. But he is too late. Just before he arrives back at his home trench, the time has run out and the men are ordered 'over the top'. With fixed bayonets they stagger across no-man's-land into the full barrage of enemy explosives, machine-gun fire – and certain death. Archy fixes his mind on his uncle's strict disciplines when he was training to be a championship runner . . . he is a runner . . . his legs are steel springs . . . he must move forward . . . he must keep going. As the picture reaches its anguished end, Archy continues running, into oblivion.

Such powerfully poignant images are tempered by moments of great fun, joy and hope for the future. Said Gibson: 'It's about deep and abiding friendship, ideals and the energy, exuberance and optimism of young people.' Creating this epic tale was a battle in itself, recalled an exhausted Weir when it was all over. 'More than 4,000 extras were used and some individual battle scenes involved 600 or 700 extras,' he explained.

Gibson agreed. 'It was almost like being in Gallipoli,' he said.

The extras were all country guys who liked a bit of fun, all believed in God and never complained, just like the country guys in World War One. They had some rough times, in trenches all day with sand kicking up in their faces, sitting in boats all night getting drenched, but they never complained. Their small roles became the most important thing to them.

Adding authority and conviction to the scene were Australian soldiers and cadets. For all concerned it was an astonishing physical achievement.

The sheer scale of *Gallipoli* meant it was never going to be the cheapest picture made. It was five years before Weir saw his vision become a reality. Many times during that period the project teetered on the brink of collapse. Even as Weir was writing the first draft the financial equations did not make sense. It was at the Cannes Film Festival in 1979 that Peter Weir rang producer Patricia Lovell to invite her to produce *Gallipoli*. She borrowed a copy of the script, said she loved it, and accepted. Twelve months later, again at Cannes where she was looking for financial backing for the picture, Weir telephoned to tell her the happy news that he had just spoken to Richard Stigwood, who wanted to go ahead with the production as he and Lovell had planned it. Stigwood, born in Australia, had left for England at twenty-one to start his own theatrical agency and later joined forces with Brian Epstein, manager of The Beatles, in NEMS Enterprises. He became a successful independent theatrical entrepreneur, presenting a number of West End productions with David Land.

At the time of *Gallipoli*, Stigwood had linked with Rupert Murdoch, forming Associated R & R Films, and was on the look-out for good scripts. He showed David Williamson's script for *Gallipoli* to Murdoch, who was immediately impressed. It was the first film backed by the new organization, but the partnership did not work out and by the time *Gallipoli* went out on release, it was virtually dissolved by mutual agreement. The picture became a $A2.8 million venture, at that time modest by Hollywood standards for an epic of its kind, and Patricia Lovell's greatest challenge.

Gallipoli was Australia's first unqualified international box-office triumph and it was generally considered that, with its release, Australian cinema came of age. It was also a resounding artistic success. When released on video it was seen as the '1981 landmark movie' for being the first to confront the most formative event in the history of Australia. One enthusiastic reviewer saw it as 'having the spectacle of *The Longest Day* and the artistry of *Chariots of Fire*'. Another described it as 'an intensely moving, beautifully-told tribute to the Anzac participation at the Dardenelles'. It was seen by one writer many years later as the picture that 'woke the world up to Australian cinema' and 'an international success which launched director Peter Weir on his Hollywood career.'

Gallipoli picked up most of the main prizes at the annual Australian Film Awards and made more money overseas than any previous Australian movie. Gibson again walked off with the Australian Film Institute's Best Actor Award. The picture did such good business in London that it beat the latest James Bond movie (though remarkably did not win a major circuit release nationwide, appearing at selected cinemas in some cities). In the United States it grossed $4 million, the best performance of any Australian film, but a different title for North American audiences would undoubtedly have boosted its success. Many Americans had never heard of Gallipoli. In Britain critics were divided, but mostly enthusiastic. *Daily Mail*: '. . . Peter Weir's magnificent film', *Daily Star*: '. . . a remarkable movie – *Gallipoli* is often funny and immensely entertaining'. *Sun*: '. . . it is a powerful and brilliant film'.

Gibson found working on *Gallipoli* an exhilarating experience. 'When I read the script I just knew it would work,' he explained. 'It has a really good theme that people can relate to. Back then, without question, people knew what they believed in – one God, honour and country.' He said he felt completely involved in it. 'I can do that when I get a truthful subject or truthful relationships to work with . . . and this film had both.'

He was understandably proud of his part in the picture and many critics believed it was his charismatic performance as the laconic 'digger' and idealistic recruit that launched his career. *Gallipoli* would certainly turn out to be a defining moment for Gibson. If left a deep and lasting impression on him and years later he would remember the smallest detail.

One of Mel's abiding memories while making *Gallipoli* is of putting a call through to Adelaide to speak to his wife Robyn, before he left his Cairo location. He was told he could not talk to her right then as she was busy. Mel had missed not having Robyn with him on location, but it was important that she stayed at home, for just at the moment Mel put his call through, Robyn was in the process of giving birth to their first child, daughter Hannah. There was too much going on for him to talk to anyone, but he insisted that the phone be left off the hook so that he was able to hear all the action, even if he could not see what was going on.

Mother, daughter – and father too it seems – were all doing

well. Later he would say that not being there at the birth was the worst mistake of his life.

6 Hollywood Takes a Hand

Mel Gibson is a natural actor. Many people, including some directors, have said so. It is a quality, alongside handsome looks, self-discipline and fortitude, which might well have carried him a fair way along the road to film stardom. But not all the way. Equally important is that he was born at the right time and in the right place.

Australia made films before World War Two, but the majority focused on homespun themes intended for indigenous audiences. When war came, facilities shut down and the industry remained dormant long after peace returned. Meanwhile the country was left to talk self-consciously about its sole film icon, the swashbuckling Errol Flynn, born in Hobart, Tasmania, but by then he was long past his prime. In the late sixties the lack of an Australian film industry became an issue of national concern and dismay. So much so that in 1970 John Gorton's government established the Australian Film Development Corporation to kickstart the revival of the industry.

So when Gibson began to think seriously about acting as a career, the country's cultural renaissance was well under way. This, along with a growing sense of national identity, brought opportunities which before had not existed for young, talented potential stars.

The second stroke of luck goes back to Hutton Gibson's decision to settle in Sydney. For it was there, within comfortable travelling distance of the family home, that the country's prestigious National Institute of Dramatic Art was located. At the time NIDA's reputation meant nothing to Mel. Nor had he even con-

sidered becoming an actor. 'But I thought I ought to give it a try,'
he later explained with little enthusiasm, completely unaware
that he would be given a better dramatic education there, virtually on his doorstep, than anywhere else in the southern hemi-
sphere.

NIDA had taken much of its lead from London's Royal
Academy of Dramatic Art (RADA) and offered an unrivalled
breadth and width of curriculum. It was not simply a question of
learning to act. Voice production and projection, gesture and
movement were also taught. So were breath control, physical
balance, mental and physical concentration and absolute discipline. At NIDA Gibson learned how to control his whole body,
how to simulate a fight, even how to sing, because singing was
important in voice production and breath control. In the class-
room he was taught the theory of acting. In the gymnasium he
learned about posture, how to control his physical movements
and how to fence. Each student had the opportunity for real acting experience. 'There was a production every three weeks and
sometimes they would deliberately miscast you, to see how you
made out,' explained Gibson. He even played Titania, Queen of
the Fairies, in Shakespeare's *A Midsummer Night's Dream*.

The tuition was mentally and physically rigorous, strongly
focused and firmly rooted in the classics. The learning process,
often tedious and repetitive, was improvisational as well as formal. Students learned to be relaxed and natural on stage. Hardly
surprising then that, countless times in the future, Mel would hit
the roof when confronted by an ill-prepared journalist who
innocently trotted out the assumption that he was a 'method
actor', the implication being that he had not gone through the
traditional mill of formal learning before emerging as a screen
star.

So if Gibson is a natural actor then it is probably as much to
do with NIDA's thorough and intensive training as through any
fluke of birth. Peter Weir was not given to long academic dis-
cussions on the whys and wherefores of Mel Gibson's talent.
The crucial point was that he could instinctively sense that
essential, indefinable star quality or potential. And after casting
Gibson in *Gallipoli* in 1980 he just knew that he wanted him
again for the lead in his next picture. Weir had been hard at
work on the preliminaries of *The Year of Living Dangerously*

(*Living Dangerously* in America) even before he directed *Gallipoli* and had made up his mind about Mel as soon as he saw him. 'I was determined to have Mel for both pictures, not just the one,' he confirmed.

But at another location director George Miller and producer Byron Kennedy were equally resolute. Once *Mad Max* began to show its paces, they quickly set about making a follow-up. Their plans hinged on Mel donning his black gear again. Only if Gibson reprised his role would American cash be forthcoming, with the proposed film being released through Warner Brothers. Mel had received just $10,000 for the first *Mad Max* picture. This time round a fee of $100,000 was being talked about. Peter Weir, meanwhile, was dangling the prospect of a $150,000 fee if Mel would only sign the contract to do *The Year of Living Dangerously*, a high-profile production due to be released through MGM/US Entertainment.

For Mel, there was only one way to resolve the dilemma. He decided to do them both.

Mad Max was in production first and this time round the concept was more clearly defined, the elements more carefully plotted. The Miller–Kennedy partnership had been established a decade before, but a meagre budget for the original *Mad Max* meant a scaling-down of some of their more imaginative ideas. Miller and Kennedy had promised each other that the original would be the one and only. *Mad Max* ended there. But when Warner Brothers came along with a cheque for $4 million they were more than happy to change their minds.

Mad Max 2, or *The Road Warrior* in the United States, was a bigger picture all round than its predecessor. Miller could let his hair down. He worked with writers Terry Hayes and Brian Hannant to produce a screenplay which was better, more carefully planned and prepared and more skilfully constructed than the original. The story took over from where the first film left off, with Max Rockatansky continuing his futuristic adventures. A nuclear holocaust has all but obliterated the world, which is now a barren and unyielding wasteland populated by a struggling band of survivors. Just as chocolate and cigarettes took over as currency in war-torn Berlin immediately after World War Two, so fuel has now become the only currency of value, the most precious commodity in the world, causing all-out war

76

between the police and bikers. There is brutal pillaging, and swiftly moving groups roam and control the highways. Max travels at hurricane speeds over a ravaged landscape.

An eloquent prologue to the new film bridged the gap between the two pictures:

> My life fades, the vision dims. All that remains are memories. They take me back . . . I remember . . . a time of chaos . . . ruined dreams . . . this wasted land. But most of all I remember the road warrior . . . the man we call Max. To understand who he was you have to go back . . . to another time . . . when the world was powered by black fuel.
>
> And the deserts sprouted great cities of pipes and steel. Gone now . . . swept away. For reasons long forgotten, two mighty warrior tribes went to war . . . and touched off a blaze that engulfed them all . . .

The entire picture was shot in and around the isolated town of Broken Hill, where zinc, lead and silver is mined, 700 miles (1150 k) west of Sydney. The area was an ideal backdrop to several films, including a TV version of *A Town Like Alice*, but the making of the *Mad Max* follow-up dominated the local scene as it was suddenly invaded by Miller's army of actors, technicians, supplies, trucks and assorted paraphernalia. There were forty cast members, almost 100 extras, eighty assorted vehicles and a camera-fitted helicopter. Medical staff and supplies were on hand as an essential precaution. Coordinating everything was a nightmare.

The basic formula was the same as the original, but the result was an altogether superior fantasy film. This time Bruce Spence, Vernon Wells and Emil Minty were acting with Gibson, but, as before, the stunts, crashes, high-speed chases and violent set-pieces were the real heroes. The enlarged budget enabled Miller to incorporate even more spectacular stunts and impressive sequences. The action is electrifying and, during ten weeks of filming, it took its toll. In the course of around 200 separate stunts, the crew wrote off more than forty cars and motorcycles. Asked about the concept of the movie, Miller explained that they were interested in telling a story appropriate to the twentieth century. Miller had a clearer mind, gained from the original, of what he wanted from the picture. He took some of his inspiration from Joseph Campbell, a leading authority on mythology who had propounded the concept that the human soul has a need of heroes. That being so, heroes are therefore created.

Gibson relished much of the high-speed driving he was allowed to do, but was barred from all the stunts. Veteran stunt driver Dennis Williams doubled for Mel in a high-speed scene which had audiences on the edge of their seats. Crouched behind nearby bushes and trees a safe distance away, cast and crew watched in heart-pounding apprehension and stark fear. Williams accelerated a mighty tanker to more than 65 m.p.h. and, having crested a rise, hurled the monster vehicle towards a bend. Aiming at a pre-determined marker up ahead, he skilfully steered the 24-wheeler crazily out of control and deliberately crashed. The vehicle rolled over, broke its back and came to rest on its side. Williams crawled out and walked away to a standing ovation.

Once again voices were raised about the level of violence in the picture. But others countered with the fact that Miller only suggested violence, did not exploit it. Mel could not see that it set a bad example or would be a bad influence on anybody.

When someone suggested it was a frightening film he replied that he saw it more as a comedy. 'Even the violence in it wasn't that brutal sort of violence. It's so far beyond reality in every way that you just can't take it seriously,' he said. 'We weren't out to make a heavy statement about a nuclear holocaust. It's just a couple of hours of exciting entertainment.' He considered George Miller had done a wonderful and creative job, adding: 'He is a true film-maker. The movie is quite straightforward and simple; it doesn't get too complex. But it takes somebody pretty talented to get that simplicity on film.'

Gibson's performance was more restrained than in the first Max picture and, as one writer pointed out, his powerfully silent presence was what made the rest of the film work. It was after this picture that George Miller announced that Mel Gibson had the potential to be one of the great actors. 'He has a screen presence and a wide range of abilities, but more than that, he seems to be deeply obsessed with the acting craft. It's a quiet, almost secret thing, but it's unmistakably there,' he said.

Though much of the filming called for 5 a.m. starts, *The Road Warrior* was a happy experience for Mel. His wife Robyn and their young baby, Hannah, were with him on location and he was always more relaxed, more contented, when surrounded by his family. The film was doing its bit turning Broken Hill into a tourist destination. At nearby Silverton, Mel's signature in the visitors' book at the local pub would soon claim almost as much attention as the town's historic jail.

The Gibsons lived in a rented house in Broken Hill, but on the set and in all aspects of making the movie, Mel enjoyed no special privileges. He was just one of the team, like everyone else. On the set Mel displayed the twin personalities for which he was becoming known – acting the fool and playing tricks when he stepped off the set, deadly serious working before the cameras. He certainly found it harder to play Max in the sequel. Not only did he have even fewer lines of dialogue than before, Miller had also given his character a harder, more detached persona. He was after a subtle kind of dramatic intensity and had no help from dialogue to achieve it. Explained Gibson: 'Max Rockatansky operated coldly because that's the only way to survive. It's down to basics. Eating dog food. Running for your life. You just live. He doesn't even sneer. He's beyond that.' It was also an arduous, tiring role physically, since Max dominates the screen for most of the film.

Gibson again worked well under Miller's astute direction, though Byron Kennedy's contribution should not be overlooked. He devised and worked out in minute detail all the breathtaking stunts, which were, of course, fundamental to the picture. Australia's stunt expert Max Aspin used to the full his experience and skill as stunt supervisor and coordinator.

Miller was confident that a good picture had emerged, despite its being probably the most complex film in technical terms ever attempted in Australia to that time. There were no certainties, however, not even for a director as skilled, creative and dedicated as Miller, who remarkably, had only one other major feature film to his name. The critics would have their say. Then the paying public would step in with their make-or-break verdict. For the first time Gibson embarked on an extensive promotional tour overseas and did a good ambassador's job, talking to the right people and saying all the right things. In Japan he was greeted enthusiastically, almost adoringly. He spent ten days there, giving a succession of interviews to newspapers and magazines, and on radio and television. The Japanese relished the all-action violence portrayed in the picture because it was reminiscent of their Samurai traditions. His tour of the United States would later provide stimulus to what was at first a sluggish response to the picture.

Meanwhile, in Britain the critics were giving their verdicts. Some raised concerns about the violence and one noted critic swam against the tide by criticizing Gibson for his 'blandness', while acknowledging that he was a 'highly accomplished screen actor'. The great majority of reviews, however, gave both Mel and the picture an impressive star rating. This was particularly the case in the important American market, where it was now essential for any major movie to do well in order to recoup funds and make a profit.

Predictably the camera wizardry and special effects claimed most of the headlines and occupied much of the meat of the reviews, though Gibson was not alone in paying tribute to the astute direction and disciplined cutting that brought added pace and tension to the picture. 'I haven't seen anyone else who can slice a picture up in quite the way he (Miller) does it,' enthused Gibson. Despite the emphasis on action and special effects it was also a picture which carried lots of suspense along with humour.

The eventual success of *The Road Warrior* was considerable and made Mel Gibson's fee for his next and seventh film significantly undervalued, even though his now firmly contracted $150,000 to do Peter Weir's *The Year of Living Dangerously* would be the biggest fee he had received. Mel had enormous respect for Weir's work and was happy to be working with him again after the success of *Gallipoli*. For his part Weir had shown every confidence in Mel's ability to handle the leading role of Guy Hamilton, an ambitious young Australian Broadcasting Service journalist undertaking his first international assignment in Indonesia and determined to make a name for himself.

Weir had identified the film possibilities in Australian writer C.J. (Chris) Koch's novel and almost immediately set about securing the film rights. That was in 1978, though he did not exercise his option until 1981 when he started filming. It would be his first big-budget picture, a landmark event for arguably Australia's most exciting director, though he was still only in his early thirties. After *Picnic at Hanging Rock* and *Gallipoli*, in which Weir had demonstrated his propensity for pyrotechnics, he returned to a story-telling movie set in the political hotbed of Indonesia in 1965.

Almost twenty years after Indonesia's liberation from the Japanese, President Achmed Sukarno talks openly of his country's political neutrality, though makes little effort to conceal his anti-British and anti-American feelings. He is suspected of widespread corruption, and conditions inside his country, with many people short of food, approach disaster levels before he is finally deposed by a military coup.

Into this threatening cauldron of intrigue, corruption and impending danger, during the final days of Sukarno's regime, steps Gibson's innocent Hamilton, confident, tough but journalistically naive. The threat of civil war between the Muslims and communists is terrifyingly real and Hamilton has been sent in by his office to gain confidence in influential places, dig out some information and write the big story. Arriving at Jakarta airport, in Java, Hamilton finds that his contact has returned to Sydney. He is suddenly on his own with no one to brief him, no foundation to work from, no on-the-ground intelligence to steer him in the right direction. He is isolated. Doors are closed to him. He finds little co-operation and can't fasten on to anything substantial. The first story he files is a tame account of Sukarno's manoeuvrings between the communists and the right-wing military that is dismissed as 'a travelogue' back at base.

His salvation comes in the form of a diminutive half-Chinese, half-Australian cameraman named Billy Kwan (actually played by a girl, Linda Hunt), who befriends him, has many useful contacts and knows his way around. Kwan helps Hamilton get the big stories other journalists miss, though inevitably the young reporter gets more and more embroiled in the political turmoil in the country, even to the point of having his leg stabbed in a communist uprising. But through Hamilton's own developing reservations, we are led to suspect Kwan. Who is he, anyway? How does he come by his inside information? Could he be a spy? We know he is an idealistic follower of President Sukarno, whom he sees as a champion of the people, with sufficient clout and craft to make things happen.

On the other hand, Hamilton's status as a foreign correspondent is considerably enhanced when Kwan arranges an exclusive interview for him with the head of the Indonesian Communist Party. The story is a scoop, rattles a few officials and politicians, and makes him a journalistic hero. It is also Kwan who introduces Hamilton to leggy Jill Bryant, assistant to the British attaché, at a swimming pool party. The two fall in love. Bryant, played by American actress Sigourney Weaver after her success in *Alien*, is a tempting distraction, but the relationship has little chance of long-term success, since she has only one week left in Java. She sees the futility of it all, but Hamilton is a tenacious suitor. In the end he must choose between his adventurous lifestyle as an international correspondent and his passion for Jill.

As *Film Review* so succinctly put it at the time: 'The audience is drawn deeper and deeper into an alien world of political unrest, animal lust and inhuman betrayal as the Communist forces rally, as Hamilton and Jill fall hopelessly in love, and as the pressures for the "story of a lifetime" mount.'

The story held so much promise in movie terms that a captivated Weir had invested his own money in the project at the outset, although the major financing was later taken over by MGM/UA. Though it was fifteen years after the dramatic events took place, it was still too recent for Weir to consider shooting in Indonesia. Instead he chose Manila, in the Philippines, to represent Jakarta because of its similarity, geographically and architecturally. But the cast and crew immediately found themselves in an atmosphere almost as explosive and hostile as that which they intended to portray in the picture. Muslim fundamentalism was on the increase round the world, after the rise of the Ayatollah Khomeini in Iran, and the Philippines was already in the grip of tension and fear.

Once in Manila Gibson and the others took little comfort from the events of the previous year, when the lives of celebrities visiting the Manila Film Festival had been threatened by a fanatical Islamist minority group. From the start of filming all the actors were assigned bodyguards. 'My bodyguard was a 6'5" Filipino, with a .38-calibre pistol under his shirt, who followed me everywhere I went,' said Mel, who could not feel entirely safe even with all doors locked in his suite at The Manila Hotel. Threats by telephone came through repeatedly: 'Get out or we will kill you.' Everyone had been made aware that there would be an element of danger once they arrived in Manila, but as it was impossible to use Jakarta as a location, it seemed no more than a reasonable risk.

Mel said that after the first phone call he wanted to leave right away. The phone rang and a voice in broken English asked how brave he was, followed by threats about bombs and death. The bodyguard snatched the phone from Gibson and yelled down the line. Then he slammed down the phone and told Mel not to worry.

'But I did worry,' explained Mel. 'I had a family, a real life, and this was only a movie.' Could they be hoaxers? someone asked, but no one was prepared to bet that they were. Weir and other members of the cast received similar threats, but no serious consequences resulted.

Gibson had been interested in doing the picture from the outset. It was a romantic drama which had something of the *Casablanca* feel to it, *Casablanca* being one of his favourite movies. He could also sense a touch of his boyhood hero, Humphrey Bogart, in the Guy Hamilton character. In any case, under Weir's direction he also rose positively to the challenge. 'He kept everything controlled,' Gibson said. 'Peter sets the scene with all the elements in place and you then go in to see what you can do with it.' This gave Gibson plenty of scope because, as he pointed out, Hamilton provided a very limited framework for an actor. 'He really was just a puppet, except when his masculine instincts took over, and seldom initiated anything. So Guy was a real challenge because there was so little to get hold of, such a narrow canvas on which to work, though he did grow a bit and gained a few insights.'

It was a different kind of role for Mel, dramatically different from *Mad Max*. He develops his character sensitively, shielding his insecurity from the other, more experienced journalists who are competing with him for the big stories. As Hamilton becomes more secure, Mel allows his character's growing confidence to ease through. Typically thorough in researching the role, Gibson spent time with journalists who had worked in Jakarta and found them a fascinating, dedicated bunch, living on the edge all the time. 'The story was all that mattered to them, the story was God,' he said.

But even the high drama of the picture had a tough time

competing with Gibson's love scenes with Sigourney Weaver, which made such an impact that they were soon being hailed as a new romantic couple. Strange, therefore, that this potential was not exploited, for they did not appear together again. The film was the first in which a Mel Gibson character falls in love, a surprising delay given his rapidly developing reputation among female audiences. Both indeed were short of love-making experience on film. Gibson was so tentative about these scenes that he called Weir to one side for advice and was sent away to study the great romantic couples like Clark Gable and Vivian Leigh, Errol Flynn and Olivia De Havilland during Hollywood's golden years. Sigourney was also nervous. More than six years older than Gibson and an inch or two taller, she had made her screen début as recently as 1976 and this political drama with Gibson was only her third film. Their anxieties, if real, proved unfounded. The love scenes were so effective and exciting that one critic, who had seen plenty of love-making on the screen, referred to their 'electrifying chemistry'. The picture would go on to make the 5 foot 11 inch red-haired Weaver a box-office star.

The most remembered romantic episode is when she is shown to be passionately attracted to Gibson, but refuses to see him again after they spend a night together. Confused, he takes the initiative at an Embassy party, backing Weaver into a corner while demanding an explanation for her changed attitude towards him. He kisses her repeatedly and insists she leaves the party with him. She is sexually much aroused, but declines. After kissing her again he walks away. Still excited, she pursues him, leaping into the car beside him as it moves off. She engulfs him with kisses and they roar away into the night. Almost as a celebration of their mutual excitement, he crashes the car into an armed road-block and the scene ends with military police shooting at the car as it disappears into the darkness.

It is an explosive scene which would be picked out time and again whenever *The Year of Living Dangerously* was reviewed or talked about. Sigourney Weaver aroused curiosity and speculation when later, asked to comment on her co-star, she said: 'Mel is the most gorgeous man I've ever seen. But people focus too much on his looks. He is also shy and a very devoted family man. And as an actor he is really extraordinarily good.'

Weaver as Jill Bryant gave a convincing portrayal of sexy elegance, her love scenes with Mel not only capturing the critics' attention but also the public's fancy. The light-hearted on-set banter, however, concerned the built-up shoes Mel was required to wear in the love encounters and the steamy swimming-pool love-scene, which was actually shot, not on location in Manila as intended, but in the safety of a welcoming, if wintry Sydney.

That return was brought forward because the situation in Manila remained stressful. Death threats continued and had now been directed at most members of the cast. Nerves were on edge, so Weir decided to head for home before the scheduled date, preferring to complete shooting, including some important scenes, in Sydney.

Linda Hunt proved a revelation as Billy Kwan, which was seen as a pivotal role and crucial to the movie's success. Weir originally had an Australian male actor in mind, but when that did not work out, a serious and urgent problem loomed. The picture was on the point of going into production, so when somebody recommended a diminutive, unknown American actress he readily agreed for her to be screen-tested. He hadn't even thought about casting a female in what was a male part, but he had seen a picture of Hunt and as her height of 4 foot 9 inches was ideal, he did a video test of her in New York, flew her to Hollywood and cast her on the spot. Only then, Hunt revealed later, did she read the script and was startled to find that her role was that of a man.

Hunt was an accomplished stage actress who had studied at the prestigious Goodman Theater School of Drama in Chicago but on film had no pedigree, though she had appeared as a prize-fighter's mother in *Popeye* in 1980. She astonished audiences with her performance as the photographer in *The Year of Living Dangerously* and the role earned her a well-deserved Oscar for Best Supporting Actress.

Peter Weir, David Williamson and Chris Koch, who had written the original book, finally shared the screenplay credits. The picture, which Gibson saw as concentrating on manipulation on both a small scale – 'that's Billy Kwan as he tries to live his life through the outer shell of Hamilton' – and on a much larger scale – 'represented by the government, the corrupt Sukarno,'

85

earned reasonably good critical reviews, though from an acting point of view it was always going to be Linda Hunt's picture. Mel finally got into the act as a co-presenter with Sissy Spacek at the famous Dorothy Chandler Pavilion venue in Los Angeles at the Academy Awards ceremonies in April 1984. Hunt made a generous speech and, holding up the famous statuette, she said '. . . I share this with him (Peter Weir) and the Filipino people, Sigourney and with Mel.'

Gibson would always be able to look back to the making of *The Year of Living Dangerously* for another special, personal reason. Once again, as during the making of *Gallipoli*, Robyn was on the point of giving birth. Mel stayed with her all night, but reported for action on the set right on time the next morning. It was on 2 June 1982 at the Women's Hospital in Crown Street, Sydney, that Mel witnessed the birth of his twins, Christian and Edward, later describing it as 'one of the happiest days of my life'.

The Year of Living Dangerously was a worthy picture, though commercially less successful than *The Road Warrior*. One suspects the story could easily have slipped away into mediocrity, finishing as a piece of trite and exploitative melodrama, but *Film Review* acknowledged the handling skills of Peter Weir. 'He applies just the right restraint to the narrative, allowing the tension of the story to build through character and atmosphere.' The picture grossed something over $8.5 million in the United States and enjoyed some critical success in Britain. It contributed to making an international star of Mel Gibson, even if it did not produce a box-office bonanza.

But Gibson would not be denied that benchmark of success, for *The Road Warrior*, was already thrilling cinema audiences, at the same time creating a new Hollywood star. One critic enthused: 'I can't define "star quality", but whatever it is, Mr Gibson has it.' The picture became a massive success – earning $24 million in the United States alone – and with huge additional earnings it would ultimately gross more than $100 million worldwide and also enjoy a significant 'cult' success over the years. Unusually, it appealed equally to audiences of both sexes.

As the handsome, American-born Aussie himself later agreed, this was the film more than any other to date that finally made mass audiences in the United States take a good look at Mel Gibson.

7   Big Cast for Bounty

The 1980s looked promising for the young Mel Gibson. *Gallipoli, The Year of Living Dangerously* and the second *Mad Max* movie had taken him to the fringes of Hollywood. A couple more good pictures – just one if he could find a blockbuster – would see him well on the way to worldwide superstardom.

The ball seemed to be rolling in the right direction when he was tipped for the lead in *The Running Man*, a fast-moving, all-action movie from Rank/Braveworld and directed by Paul Michael Glaser, of *Starsky and Hutch* television fame. The picture was about to go into pre-production when a call from Gibson's American agent, Ed Limato, advised him to hold off. He had a more attractive project lined up, one which offered not only more cash but which Limato was confident would make his client an international star.

The new picture was an updated version of the legendary adventure story *Mutiny on the Bounty*, which could easily stand another telling. Based on the book *Captain Bligh and Mr Christian* by Richard Hough, the twice Oscar-winning screenwriter Robert Bolt had produced a completely new script, and the venture had good financial backing. Already lined up for the new movie were established major British stars Anthony Hopkins, Laurence Olivier, Edward Fox and Bernard Hill, along with Daniel Day-Lewis after an unnoticed appearance in *Gandhi*. So Gibson signed up to *The Bounty*, while his part in *The Running Man* was eventually taken over by Arnold Schwarzenegger.

Despite all the early promise and optimism, the picture failed to elevate Gibson's career and worked against his best interests at a personal level, too. Mel had been drinking with growing

enthusiasm of late and a nine-week shoot on the remote paradise
island of Moorea, near Tahiti, under a relentless sun and with little to occupy the time between bouts of filming, was not exactly calculated to induce temperance. Co-star Anthony Hopkins
though resolutely on the wagon later claimed that being a close
witness to Gibson's drinking bouts was hard on his own absti-
nence. But without the restraining influence from Robyn, who
found it impossible to accompany her husband with their children into such a remote area for so long, the temptations for
Mel were strong.

In the role of the mutinous Fletcher Christian, Gibson was
following in the footsteps of such legendary characters as Errol
Flynn, in his screen debut (1932), Clark Gable (1935) and
Marlon Brando (1962). In fact he had secured the role after both
Sting and Christopher Reeve, among others, had been tipped for
the lead. Reeve was actually selected, but pulled out a few weeks
before shooting was due to begin. Reeve had actually been cast
very early on, when distinguished British film director David
Lean was the guiding force behind the project. Lean had stum-
bled on the idea of what would be a fifth telling of the classic
tale (there had been an ancient silent version) after travelling to
Tahiti with a completely different plan, a picture based on the
life of British explorer Captain Cook. Thereafter, the birth
pangs of this latest Bounty story were both painful and complicated. Having switched course, Lean managed to secure crucial
financial backing from Warner Brothers and then brought in his
friend Robert Bolt to work on a script. But when the studio later
withdrew from the project, the Italian producer Dino de
Laurentiis stepped in with even more ambitious plans and a virtually open cheque-book.

De Laurentiis, then in his mid sixties, had been in the business
for years and was remembered for his collaboration on film projects in the 1950s with the renowned Carlo Ponti. His penchant
for overblown international productions had probably started in
1979 with *Hurricane*, an extravagant remake of the 1937 South
Sea island Dorothy Lamour–Jon Hall classic *The Hurricane*, but
this time starring Jason Robards and Mia Farrow. His vision for
the new Bounty picture was customarily extravagant by any
standards.

In fact he and Lean decided to reinvent the story through two

89

associated pictures, not just a single movie. Lean subsequently withdrew, fearing that this extended ambition was now seriously in danger of carrying them all into rough and uncharted seas. The project fell dormant until Hollywood's Orion Pictures decided to finance a new single Bounty picture and brought in New Zealander Roger Donaldson as director. Reeve, by this time unsettled by all the changes and uncertainty, decided to pull out. Only then did the door open for Mel Gibson to take over.

In many ways this latest picture would be seen as the best and most seriously intended version so far of this sea-faring classic. Gone was much of the synthetic melodrama of earlier versions as Bolt's script had the events unfolding simply and convincingly. A big budget had been set aside for the picture and preliminary arrangements suggested care and trouble would be taken to make sure the treatment was authentic. An impressive replica of HMS *Bounty*, which had been painstakingly constructed at the start of the picture's gestation period – five whole years before filming started – alone cost producer Dino De Laurentiis well in excess of $2 million. The famous Italian-born film-maker was clearly determined to maintain his reputation for productions on a grandiose scale. From the outset *The Bounty* was sure to be a film of epic proportions. With a starting budget of around $20 million, a resounding box-office response was essential if the film was to be a financial success.

The project eventually got underway in the latter part of April 1983 with a few early scenes based on the story's famous court-martial being shot in London. Then Gibson, Hopkins and the others flew off to Papeete, the capital city of French Polynesia, for their nine-week stay in paradise. The film would then be completed in New Zealand, where the final few scenes were shot.

Life on Moorea was at first paradise on earth for both cast and crew. Its tall, swaying palms, wonderful coral sand beaches and picturesque bays, warm and comforting sunshine created a lilting and gentle pace to life. But a down side developed, too. High winds and hurricanes battered the film-makers' carefully constructed sets, but ironically it was during a man-made storm sequence that Gibson was blown completely off his feet. Organizing large numbers of inexperienced extras also proved a problem. And, as Hopkins commented, 'Even paradise can wear a bit thin after a time.'

In such relaxed surroundings, and with little else to do when not filming, nothing was more natural than to sink a few beers. But the situation got out of hand. Reports filtered through of heavy drinking bouts, pub skirmishes and a fight with locals in which Gibson was said to have been involved. Evidence came in the form of nasty bruises and abrasions down one side of his face, which had to be kept out of camera view for a few days while cameramen took their shots from different angles.

Based on the real-life events of more than 200 years before, this latest version rejected the well-established formula of clearly defined heroes and villains set against an idealized South Seas paradise. Captain Bligh wasn't such a monster after all, it was decided; nor was Fletcher Christian the unblemished hero of old. Playing his part in alerting the public to the new spin on the old yarn, Gibson explained: 'I'll be playing Christian as the manic-depressive paranoid schizophrenic that he really was.' Hopkins also nailed his flag to the mast. 'This Bligh, this story, is the more accurate version,' he proclaimed.

But *The Bounty*, if nothing else, would prove that you cannot play fast and loose with well-loved and solidly established legends, however well-intentioned; and certainly not when those legends are set against the romanticized, idyllic paradise of the South Seas. Too much realism can spoil the dream, and the public is not always happy about that.

Just to remind ourselves of the real story: Captain William Bligh (1754–1817), was a British admiral who accompanied Cook on his second voyage round the world and in 1787 was sent to Tahiti on HMS *Bounty* to collect specimens of the breadfruit tree. After setting sail for home, and just a few days out from Tahiti, Bligh's crew mutinied against the tyrannical conduct of their commander and deserted, casting off the admiral and eighteen officers in a small boat without maps. Against all the odds the pugnacious Bligh, in a masterly display of seamanship, eventually sailed his small boat some 3,600 miles (6,000 kilometres) before reaching the safety on Timor, north of Australia.

Meanwhile, the mutineers, led by Fletcher Christian, put back into Tahiti, where most of them decided to settle. Nine of them, however, sailed for Pitcairn Island, 1,200 miles south east of Tahiti, accompanied by some of the native women. The following year, Captain Edwards of HMS *Pandora* captured twelve of

91

the mutineers at Tahiti and hanged three of them. The fate of those who sailed for Pitcairn remained unknown until 1808, when an American vessel touching there found the island inhabited by a mixed-race community, comprising the children of the *Bounty* mutineers and their native wives, which was ruled by John Adams, the last surviving sailor from the mutiny, who lived until 1829.

The film dramatizes the events stylishly and perceptively, the story emerging in a series of flashbacks: the opening sequences show Captain William Bligh arriving at the court martial in London which took place a year after the mutiny erupted.

We see the full-masted splendour of the departure of HMS *Bounty* from England on 23 December 1787, bound for Tahiti – and for troubled water. Tensions build as the irascible Bligh replaces his quarrelsome second-in-command John Fryer (Daniel Day-Lewis) with his then friend Fletcher Christian. An unexpectedly long stay of six months on Tahiti, while the crew wait for the breadfruit to cultivate, makes them lazy, undisciplined and insubordinate. They have grown used to the relaxing sun, the sexually willing native women and the cool blue lagoons of their island paradise. When the time comes to leave, Bligh has to bring them back in line with increased discipline; hence, eventually, the mutiny.

Gibson had expressed some doubts about the picture when he first read the script. He was convinced that Christian was being portrayed as too weak a character, who seemed to feature only sporadically. Nor was he sure he wanted to do a picture whose story had already been told in popular sound films three times already, despite this being a departure from the standard interpretation.

Once on the island location in the rough-and-tumble of filming, Gibson could find little consolation in the nightly rushes, which he said only heightened his doubts about the final result. His disenchantment might possibly be traced to the painstaking research into his character that he had carried out in Britain. To enable him to delve beneath the conventional view of Fletcher Christian, he had consulted a London psychiatrist to assess different aspects of his character's life and had even visited the house in the Lake District where Christian was born. He felt he knew a Fletcher Christian who was different to the one conveyed in the script.

But as an actor trying to make his way in the business, there was little he could do, though some eyebrows were raised on the set when he began to improvise here and there. The mutiny sequence, where Christian informs Bligh that he is taking over the ship, is the picture's moment of big drama and Gibson was determined not to squander the impact. As the cameras rolled everyone was aghast, including Hopkins who shared the scene with him, when they realized that Gibson had virtually rewritten the scene.

On a separate level, De Laurentiis unwittingly exacerbated the situation by casting a beautiful native girl straight out of high school as Gibson's love interest. Tevaite Vernette was just eighteen and had not acted before. She was ambitious to enter law and had no thoughts of becoming an actress. Nor did she have much experience of life. It was hardly surprising that some of her love scenes with Mel proved difficult for her to handle, particularly since she was not unaffected by such close contact with one of Hollywood's most handsome and desirable men. Her inexperience also made it hard for her to reconcile the love and close physical attention of the leading man when playing a scene with the cameras rolling, with his detached, almost dismissive attitude immediately shooting was over. She reportedly found her topless scene in the lagoon particularly difficult. First, her embarrassment in some of the early, perhaps clumsy takes was so obvious that her shyness became heightened; and second, she was said to have been openly criticized by some older local women, who claimed she had degraded the Tahitian race by allowing her breasts to be shown in such a way.

But she was beautifully cast in the part, producing a convincing blend of natural innocence and youthful desire. Despite being targeted with further film offers that would have made her extremely rich, she made sure that *The Bounty* was her one and only moment in the spotlight. She never appeared in front of the cameras again, opting for a career as a nurse in a post-operative care unit at an island hospital. 'There is more to life than just being in films,' she proclaimed some years later.

This well constructed and, in many ways, compelling version of a well-known story had promised much and in many respects achieved a great deal. There were exemplary performances from

93

a superb cast. The cameo role of Sir Laurence Olivier as the Lord High Admiral was a masterly piece of casting and Anthony Hopkins's portrayal as a tortured but more humanized Bligh was judged by some to surpass Charles Laughton's famous interpretation almost fifty years earlier in the Academy Award-winning MGM picture. As the handsome, underplayed, Fletcher Christian, Mel Gibson did his growing reputation as a new screen idol no harm whatsoever, despite the lukewarm verdict delivered by some major reviewers. The settings were superb and the picture was impressively photographed. The music, composed and performed by Vangelis, was sensitive to the changing moods of the movie.

A big promotional budget heralded the arrival of *The Bounty* on both sides of the Atlantic. Posters and press advertisements whetted the appetite with tempting straplines: 'They began their epic voyage as friends . . . it ended in hatred and bloodshed'; and 'After 200 years, the truth behind the legend'. In London the picture was granted the accolade of a Royal Charity Premiere at the ABC Shaftesbury Avenue in the presence of the Duke and Duchess of Kent. All seats sold out in advance.

Yet *The Bounty* was a commercial failure, with the all-important North American box office grossing less than half the budgeted cost of the picture and only a fraction of the final estimated expenditure. Some critics did not help its chances of success with trenchant verdicts like, 'A long voyage to nowhere', and 'This misshapen movie doesn't work as an epic – it doesn't have the scope or the emotional surge' and 'Bounty misses the boat'. Others slated Gibson's performance, which suffered against Hopkins' convincing interpretation of Bligh. Even his big-scene rewrite failed to impress. Back in Australia is was mercilessly torn apart by Philippa Hawker in the prestigious *Cinema Papers*: 'Just before Mel puts Bligh into the lifeboat, he erupts into a raving frenzy, an outpouring of hysteria which breaks his voice and gives us precisely nothing.' There were some good verdicts too, but they were too thin on the ground and insufficiently enthusiastic to persuade cinemagoers to pass through the box office.

Gibson made little official comment about the commercial failure of *The Bounty*. He probably felt there was little constructive to be said. And in any event, his mind was focused on the immediate future. New York-born director Mark Rydell had been waiting impatiently for Gibson to unhitch himself from the South Seas saga before making a serious start on *The River*, in which he had Gibson co-starring with Sissy Spacek. And after that Gibson was scheduled to do *Mrs Soffel* with director Gillian Armstrong. Unfortunately neither would give him the positive breakthrough that Gibson and others in the business sensed was just around the corner.

The River was a total departure for Gibson. For the first time he would be making a picture in the United States, financed by an American studio. For the first time he would be playing the role of an American citizen, in a 'family' film that upheld slightly fading, old-world values like the transmission of skills and traditions from fathers to sons, mothers to daughters. Said Rydell: 'It's about one family's dogged fight to hold on in the face of the pressure of nature and a failing economy.'

If all this sounds dreary and commonplace compared with the driving physical energy and the basic instincts of *Mad Max*, perhaps that's why the picture failed to take off at the box office. Yet *The River* was a worthy picture. Gibson and Spacek play small-time farmers Mr and Mrs Garvey, a devoted couple with two children, Shane Bailey and little Becky Jo Lynch. 'Exposed to the awesome power of nature, the Garveys are further threatened by mounting debts and the sinister plans of big business,' said Rydell. 'It's a spectacular, yet sensitive human drama; it's about the lifestyle that made America work.' Happily, Tom and Mae triumph in the end.

Simply to dismiss *The River* as an old-fashioned rural drama with a dash of symbolism would be to do it a huge injustice. The picture is superbly crafted, the characters are intelligently portrayed and the plot is directed with a fine sense of pace by Rydell. The devoted Garveys lead a tough life as they battle against the largely infertile soil and the rushing, unyielding power of the nearby river when the heavy rains bring flooding, sometimes twice a year, to threaten their crops. There are stunningly photographed moments offering intense human drama. The two flood sequences are riveting high-spots. Rydell explained how they had worked out the footage of both in precise detail, one to be shot during darkness. But flooding water is not always easy to control, even when Hollywood, with all its resources, is calling the shots.

Gibson, Spacek and the children faced the physical exertion and discomfort with fortitude. As they battle to save their farm, Sissy and the youngsters are seen filling sandbags with demonic zeal while Mel struggles to control the high-revving bulldozer, scooping and pushing up mud to reinforce a rapidly disintegrating embankment.

The family bond holds firm in the face of government support for a major agricultural cartel determined to secure the Garveys' birthright by whatever means necessary. As Gibson pointed out: 'Their life becomes threatened, not just by the awesome power of nature, but by the equally dangerous and sinister plans of big business.' The cartel is fronted by the handsome Scott Glenn, who, as the prosperous, devious and relentless enemy, attempts to tear the family apart by seducing Mae Garvey.

When casting the picture former jazz pianist Mark Rydell, already adept in the presentation of human dramas and Oscar-nominated for his *On Golden Pond* (1981), had been reluctant to consider Gibson as a possible Tom Garvey. 'He looked upon him too much as an Australian in both accent and ways and who, as an actor, still had some way to go before being accepted internationally,' said one observer. But Mel was determined.

The role called for the accurate inflections of a small-scale farmer born and bred in Tennessee – not difficult for co-star Sissy Spacek, who had been born in Texas, but a tough proposition for a New York-born Australian. Rydell had grave doubts. But Mel impressed Rydell with his strong conviction that he could play Tom Garvey successfully and even managed to elicit a promise from the director not to cast the part finally until Gibson returned from Tahiti. Meanwhile, in London to shoot some footage for *The Bounty*, Mel spent time with a voice coach specializing in dialects, working hard on the specific southern American accent required. When he later read parts of the script for Rydell the director was astonished and delighted. 'Gibson was right for the part,' he concluded. Gibson's selection, according to a studio insider, irritated Harrison Ford, who was said to have fancied the part for himself.

Gibson was calm and controlled during the making of *The River*, in stark contrast with his recent time in Tahiti. He said how much he had enjoyed the experience. He and Sissy Spacek – whose performance was nominated for an Academy Award –

Catherine Hill Bay, the location of Mel Gibson's first-ever movie, *Summer City* (1978)

Early learning centre for schoolboy Mel – St Leo's College, Sydney, Australia

Hollywood star Piper Laurie was impressed with the sensitive portrayal of Mel Gibson in *Tim* (1980)

With co-star Joanne Samuel in a scene from *Mad Max* (1980). The picture became the most successful Australian movie ever, at that time, and brought Mel stardom in his first featured role

With Mark Lee in *Gallipoli*, one of the most impressive films ever made by the Australian film industry. Released in 1981 it was a picture of epic proportions

With Feral Kid (Emil Minty) driving an oil tanker into the heart of the enemy camp in *Mad Max: The Road Warrior* (1982)

Pictured with director Peter Weir, who had also directed *Gallipoli*, and co-star Sigourney Weaver on the set of *The Year of Living Dangerously* (1983)

The spectacular human drama *The River* (1984) featuring Sissy Spacek as co-star in a battle against floods and foes

As Fletcher Christian in the ambitious and heavily financed exotic island adventure *The Bounty* (1984). Little wonder Mel Gibson acquired the title of 'The Sexiest Man Alive'

Tevaite Vernette was the native love interest in *The Bounty*. Gibson followed in the footsteps of Gable, Brando and Flynn in playing sea-faring mutineer Fletcher Christian

The grim melodramatic *Mrs Soffel* (1984) featuring Mel Gibson as a young handsome jailbird and prison governor's wife Diane Keaton as the older woman

With co-star Tina Turner in *Mad Max Beyond Thunderdome* (1985)

In the action thriller *Tequila Sunrise* (1988) Michelle Pfeiffer is a woman caught between two long-time friends whose lives take different directions: police lieutenant Nick Frescia (Kurt Russell) and drug dealer Dale McKussic (Mel Gibson)

Mel Gibson and Danny Glover, one of the most successful screen partnerships of modern times, in *Lethal Weapon 2* (1989). They starred in three *Lethal Weapon* movies which in total grossed more than $370 million in the United States alone

In the 1990 movie *Bird on a Wire* Mel Gibson and Goldie Hawn are former lovers whose romance is re-ignited when they are plunged into a cross-country run for their lives

Mel Gibson, seldom far away from his jokey fun-loving image, with Goldie Hawn in *Bird on a Wire*

were mutually complimentary. Mel benefited from having Robyn and their three children with him, all comfortably settled in a large rented house in nearby Kingsport for the duration of the shooting. Mel's children and Sissy's small daughter were sometimes allowed on the set. 'They were all great pals,' explained Sissy, 'but too young to remain silent. So we had to keep doing retakes.'

With the film completed Rydell was optimistic about its chances at the box office and heaped praise on Gibson's performance, crediting him with the roughness of Steve McQueen and the gentleness of Montgomery Clift. Reviews for *The River* were mixed. While Spacek's performance was generally praised, Gibson was widely considered to be a 'developing' actor, one showing promise. The film didn't set the world alight, but it certainly did much better business than *The Bounty*.

Gibson had little time to ponder the verdicts, even though he felt the picture represented his best performance of his career and he was disappointed by the public response. Long before *The River* was released he began work with co-star Diane Keaton on a new picture called *Mrs Soffel*, shooting on location in the wintry cold of Canada. He had taken on the commitment long before finishing work on *The River*, claiming he was attracted to the opportunity of working with director Gillian Armstrong on a $15 million project based on a true and dramatic story with a tragic ending.

The story concerns the fate of brothers Ed (played by Gibson) and Jack Biddle (Matthew Modine), known robbers who had been sentenced to death by hanging for the murder of a grocer during a bungled burglary. Kate Soffel, played by Diane Keaton, is a caring and compassionate woman, disillusioned and frustrated by her marriage with the warder of the Allegheny County Jail in Pittsburgh, where the brothers are being held. She tempers her sad and lonely existence by spending much of her time looking after the well-being of the gaol's inmates. She provides Bibles and blankets, helps with difficult letters that need to be written and generally brings a touch of humanity and concern into the wrecked lives of the desperate souls who occupy the cells. She becomes attracted to Gibson's character and Mel, scheming, manipulative and desperate, skilfully plays on her emotions, gaining her respect, confidence, even love, until she agrees to help him and his brother escape.

Gillian Armstrong, an Australian director of some standing, was an all-round professional with an equal reputation as a screenwriter and producer. She wrote, produced and directed her first film in 1971. Seven years later Armstrong's ongoing professional preoccupation with the lives of free-thinking, independent women brought her critical acclaim with the release of *My Brilliant Career*. This, her first major feature film, won seven AFI (Australian Film Institute) awards and the British Critics' Award for the best first feature. Four years later her second feature, *Starstruck*, a new-wave musical, brought her to the attention of Hollywood. She was bombarded with scripts, but nothing appealed to her until, after being invited to Los Angeles to discuss future prospects, a friend sent her a couple of ideas to consider. That friend was Hollywood star Diane Keaton, and *Mrs Soffel* was the result.

Armstrong was looking for a project which would bring her that all-important breakthrough in Hollywood. Keaton was seeking the rekindling of a career which had gone lukewarm after her success in both *Annie Hall*, some six years earlier, and *Reds*, for which she gained an Academy Award nomination. *Mrs Soffel*, backed by MGM/UA, looked a bright contender and well capable of turning the key for both of them.

It was a powerful story given greater depth by the characterizations of the main players. A well-meaning dedicated Christian, Kate Soffel endures a humdrum and disenchanted life with an uncaring husband who has long since lost any feelings for her and pays her little attention. Her compassionate instinct to help inmates gives her life a narrow purpose. She cares for her four children, but is unhappy and vulnerable. She responds innocently to the friendship of the two convicted brothers and is later flattered when the handsome Ed Biddle (Gibson), twelve years younger than herself, becomes affectionate towards her. She becomes excited, consumed and responsive as they are drawn together physically. By the time Ed and his brother break out of gaol Kate, who has effected their release by smuggling a hacksaw into their cell hidden inside a Bible flees with the brothers as they make their escape under cover of darkness, leaving behind her unloving husband, dreary lifestyle and children.

The grim, melodramatic tale follows the relentless pursuit of the fugitives as they travel north into Canada. There the two brothers are gunned down, and Kate survives, despite begging Ed to shoot her. In a twisted kind of irony, she pays for her deed by being held in the cell from which she had helped the brothers to escape.

From the start Armstrong wanted Mel Gibson for her powerful, romantic drama, but it was a long time, and only after a good deal of scheming, before she could put the idea to him, so well was he now protected by agents and minders. But once he read the script he was keen to do the picture; for him a good script is one he can read right through in one sitting. And for Armstrong, all her time, frustration, effort and anxiety was more than rewarded by seeing Mel's signature on the contract. 'Mel has this special quality which allows him to be both dangerous and romantic at the same time ... and that is rare,' she explained.

The making of *Mrs Soffel* was a tough and frustrating experience for the cast and crew. Many of the protracted and physically demanding outdoor sequences had to be filmed in freezing temperatures on snowy ground in Canada. Often the weather was unpredictable. One relatively simple scene took Armstrong an entire week to complete. Vital co-operation at a couple of important locations was unexpectedly withheld for a time. Inevitably the schedules slipped and studio executives in Hollywood, with a keen eye on the picture's $15 million budget, demanded that Armstrong speed up filming and keep costs under control. The situation became so serious, some insiders revealed, that the project was thrown into turmoil. Armstrong insisted on shooting the important death-row scenes authentically inside the Pittsburgh prison which had housed the real-life Mrs Soffel and the Biddle brothers. But this meant moving the production unit, which would be expensive, and settling a dispute with inmates and warders about fees. Little wonder studio executives urged Armstrong to use any convenient gaol close to hand. But Armstrong, supported by Gibson and Keaton, won the battle.

Earlier, while shooting scenes in Canada, Gibson had thrown everyone into a high state of panic by driving his Pontiac into the back of 23-year-old Randy Caddell's car while he was stationary at a stop light. He was held by police on a drink-drive charge. With their multi-million dollar project at risk if Mel was sentenced to time in prison, the studio dispatched a top lawyer to plead his case. By this time Caddell, whose car was not badly damaged, was calmer. He now realized who the Pontiac driver was and did not wish to make a big deal over the incident. So on 2 May 1984 Gibson pleaded guilty to the charge before the Ontario Provincial Court judge, George Carter. Much depended on the next few minutes. Gibson's lawyer pointed out that the alcohol levels were 'on the low side'. Fortunately, the judge agreed. The lawyer reminded the court that Gibson had no previous convictions and that he had expressly asked him (the lawyer) to convey to the court his (Gibson's) commendation of the arresting police officer for his courtesy and polite manner. Then the judge passed sentence which brought intense relief to the faces of the film-makers: a fine of $C300 and a three-month withdrawal of Gibson's driving licence.

To Mel's irritation, the incident received almost as much coverage, and certainly bigger headlines, back in Australia as the later release of *Mrs Soffel*. In America *Mrs Soffel* was released just a few days after *The River* and just in time to qualify for the Academy Award nominations. But despite attracting some good reviews and gaining widespread respect for its sensitive approach and meaty content, *Mrs Soffel* would never be in the running for a big award. In the end, it struggled to make $4 million at the box office.

8 Close to the Edge

In October 1984, in the small Suffolk town of Woodbridge, Timothy Jupp had something on his mind. He wanted to know if there was going to be a *Mad Max 3* and, if so, whether the picture was already in production. It seemed unlikely, according to the experts on a well-known film magazine, because *Mad Max* producer Byron Kennedy had been killed in an air crash the year before and Mel Gibson was said to be enjoying a lucrative career in the United States.

But unfolding events would show that Timothy Jupp had no cause for concern. Perhaps the reason for his anxiety was that Kennedy and director George Miller had announced as early as June 1983 that they were planning a third adventure for their big-screen hero. The further exciting news, Miller explained, was that *Mad Max 3*, which would become *Mad Max Beyond Thunderdome* would represent a 'quantum leap' over its immediate predecessor with a budget possibly reaching $8 million – double that of *The Road Warrior*. Fans of the intrepid warrior were obviously in for a treat.

Then the project fell ominously silent.

Kennedy's premature death aged thirty-three, within just a few weeks of those first announcements, was caused when his helicopter, with himself at the controls, crashed into Lake Burragorang, just south of Sydney. The tragedy was a massive blow and doubtless blanketed the project for a time. But Miller was determined to go forward with the ambitious plan they had jointly put together, having declared some time before that the main reason for bringing Max back for a third adventure was because of his own 'personal obsession' with the character. He would now assume the role of producer himself, while continuing as director to handle all the vital action sequences for which the *Mad Max* movies had become renowned. He then brought in an additional director, the well-known Australian stage director George Ogilvie, an old and trusted colleague, to supervise the acting.

It was an emotional occasion, not least for Mel Gibson, when the new picture finally went into production in September 1984, only four months later than the estimated start date. Just a year before, while on location in Tennessee working on *The River*, he had been honoured to announce to the audience at the annual Australian Film Awards ceremony, via satellite link, the inauguration of an annual Byron Kennedy Award. It was intended to stand as a lasting memorial to a man who had not only made an enormous contribution to the world of Australian film and to Gibson's own movie career in particular, but someone who had also become a good friend.

As shooting started on the new picture, thoughts were inevitably of Kennedy and the significant contribution he had made to the outstanding success of the earlier *Mad Max* pictures. Though Gibson was naturally the automatic choice for the starring role, he was not fired up to do it. Both physically and psychologically, he felt drained and detached, and was finding life difficult. Film-making had taken over his life, one picture relentlessly following the next; sometimes they even overlapped. *The Bounty, The River* and *Mrs Soffel*, all demanding long and exhausting periods of location work, would be released within the incredibly short space of one year. It seemed inconceivable that only six years earlier he had taken those awkward steps into a movie career in the low-budget *Summer City*. Even more astonishing was that nine mainstream Mel Gibson pictures had been released between 1980 and 1984. No contemporary professional actor had inflicted on himself such a punishing programme. It was a crippling regime and he was paying the price. He was irritable, quarrelsome and bad-tempered. The twinkling eyes and fun personality had gone. He had been drinking and smoking excessively. Just a few weeks spent happily at home with Robyn and the children, though contentedly and mildly therapeutic, would prove much too short a convalescence.

George Miller was calling for his return. *Mad Max Beyond Thunderdome* was waiting to go into production. Gibson's instincts told him he needed the rest more than the rigours of making yet another picture. But those same instincts also reminded him that acting was a speculative and insecure profession for someone with a wife and growing family to support; that for a movie actor it is easy to disappear from view and be lost forever. And he still felt he had a long way to go in his career. Warner Brothers had already provisionally set aside more than $5 million to make the movie, and Gibson knew they were dangling a tempting $1 million fee for him to become Mad Max once more. So he recharged his tired limbs, shrugged away his mental weariness, and in doing so found himself stuck out in a God-forsaken part of Australia's outback with weeks of unappetizing location work stretching out ahead of him.

George Miller and his associate Terry Hayes had combined to produce a screenplay which, retaining a core of the Mad Max persona from the first two movies, was also significantly different. Miller credits his co-writer with these important developments. 'Terry mentioned an idea for a story he had in mind for Max which centred on a tribe of feral children in a remote corner of the world, waiting for a legendary lost leader,' he said. 'It was then that I realized we were talking about the next chapter in the *Mad Max* saga.'

A different saga it certainly was. For a start, Mel's co-star, raunchy rock-singer Tina Turner, had not featured in the earlier incarnations. And, as *Photoplay* declared at the time, 'our hero shows discreet signs of humanity' which might well have alarmed hardcore *Mad Max* fans. The magazine reassured readers, however, that the movie had much else to commend it including 'quirky violence, a gallery of Antipodean grotesques and, of course, Mel Gibson.'

Mad Max Beyond Thunderdome certainly thrust our hero into a totally new orbit. He had evolved from the nihilism of the first picture, through the over-riding survival instincts of the second; and now, with this latest reincarnation, he emerged as the pivotal character in a new kind of society – one that has arisen out of an earlier, destroyed civilization, whose only evidence is the remnants of modern technology left scattered on the planet. Ancient rituals have been resurrected, but refined with mechanical ingenuity in a chaotic market city called Bartertown, a disjointed collection of tumbledown huts in an old mine pit, where

103

anything is subject to trade, from a sip of water to a human life. The fresh handling, perhaps owing a touch to *Star Wars*, would broaden its appeal and extend its box-office life.

The centre of attraction in this post-apocalyptic city is the Thunderdome, where old scores are settled in historic gladiatorial fashion and the public entertained in a style even more basic and robust than that of ancient Rome. The rules are simple and never change: two men enter, one man leaves. The architect of this lethal sport is the superficial ruler of Bartertown, the powerful yet alluring Aunty Entity, the redoubtable Tina Turner, resplendent in a fetching 'hang-loose' chainmail-style outfit complete with deep cleavage, a longish blonde wig and saucy French-style suspenders. Thunderdome, as Entity points out in the film, 'is where there's no jury, no appeal and no parole'. It is simply a place where all weapons are fair and there are no rules.

Gibson explained: 'In the first film Max was a cop, a relatively normal guy who descended into hell when those closest to him were killed. By the time he became the *Road Warrior*, he was a kind of closet human being, whose sole instinct was to survive. But in *Thunderdome* they've lifted the lid and let the character emerge.' He admitted that without some kind of development in his character – and for Gibson that simply meant giving Max more depth and humanity – he would not have done the picture. 'What would've been the point?' he added. 'But this is a much more human story, even though it has that same kinetic energy.' Above all he considered the third Max to have greater creative possibilities. 'Until now he was almost a cardboard cut-out, a strip cartoon, a comic book hero, but with *Mad Max 3* there was the chance to shape the character, to give it a dimension.'

Miller said he had never really anticipated making the second Mad Max picture, let alone a third. What brought him to it was the realization that the intrepid Max was an archetypal hero, part of a tradition that goes back through centuries of storytelling. 'It is only the outer guise that is different,' he explained, 'from the wandering samurai to the solitary gunslinger, to the traveller in space.' There was, of course, another, more commercial reason. Original ideas are hard to come by and the astonishing success of the earlier Max pictures, put together on a modest budget, meant that Hollywood was exerting huge pressure to bring him back again.

Tina Turner was an inspired choice as a kind of warrior queen. She plays her unconventional villain with style, vitality, intelligence; though at times predictable, she has the right combination of aggression and calm authority to make her control over Bartertown credible. 'We wanted a very positive character for the role, rather than a conventional, evil "bad guy" and someone who was overtly sexual,' explained Miller. Later he revealed that he and Hayes had someone like Turner in mind when working on the script, though she had never really acted before. She quickly put that right by arriving in Australia well ahead of filming to attend a series of acting workshops.

Another quirky, but crucial location in the film, beyond Bartertown and its Thunderdome, is the Crack in the Earth, a deep canyon inhabited by a tribe of wild children led by the striking Helen Buday, an unknown German–Hungarian actress–dancer making her screen debut. Descended from the survivors of a much earlier airplane crash they await the return of their Messiah, the long-dead Captain Walker, who piloted the crashed plane. Legend tells them that one day he will lead them to a bright and promising future. When they come across a half-dead Mad Max in the desert, they are certain the waiting is over.

One early climax in the story is the showdown in the Thunderdome between Mad Max and Aunty Entity's traditional enemy and the underworld boss of Bartertown, Master Blaster. The crafty Aunty has cunningly stage-managed the encounter after first meeting Max, about whom she feels wary, even suspicious. When he triumphs over the crossbows and axes of her henchmen Aunty is impressed and, more to the point, sees Max as a means of overcoming her arch-enemy.

Blaster is a composite freak – a helmeted and dim-witted Goliath, upon whose shoulders sits a brainy dwarf called Master. Entity's plan is to destroy the brawn element and keep the brain for herself, and she manoeuvres Max into an elaborate and grossly uneven combat with the enormously powerful Blaster. The contest takes centre stage at Thunderdome and the film's already unreal quality is jacked up with the contest's bizarre public introduction, addressed to a packed and excited house: 'Ladies and gentlemen, boys and girls, dyin' time is here.'

The honest Max has agreed to the encounter only on the basis that the contest will be strictly fair, but Aunty Entity knows that

105

he will be completely overwhelmed on that basis; and in any event, she wishes to eliminate Max as well. Against all the odds, Max gains the upper hand by blowing hard on a whistle, which sends Blaster grabbing for his ears and leaving himself open to Max, who then shows he is too nice a guy to finish him off. When one of her henchmen does the deed by firing his crossbow into Blaster, Aunty announces to the bloodthirsty crowd that as Max has broken the sacred rule by not fighting to the death, he must pay the price. The burlesque continues. He had broken the law and, as Aunty Entity points out to everyone, the law says, 'Bust a deal – face the wheel.' The wheel, like a relic from an old-time television game show, will seal Max's fate when the arrow spins round and comes to rest. His fate is to be cast out into the desert and there to die. But he doesn't, of course, and there is much more rather complicated fantasy after he is saved by the children and before the picture ends with him striding away from the camera and into the sunset. It is an appropriate ending for the Mad Max character. It could mark his permanent demise, but equally it permits him to return in some other form, some time in the future. The picture was put out as a Kennedy–Miller production and a dedication at the end of the credits stated simply: 'For Byron.'

The huge, purist army of 'Mad Maxers' who would feel grossly cheated if their hero had, this time round, forsaken two-, four-, or multiple-wheel vehicular adventures, were not to be denied, though were kept waiting nervously until nearly the end. But when those thrilling action sequences do finally blast on to the screen, with over twenty vehicles taking part, they more than compensate for the hold-up. The spectacular high-speed, head-on collision and consequent traffic mayhem against a vista of open desert is breathtaking.

The dimly lit sets and deep, dark shadows used to create the grim, unyielding atmosphere of the first part of the picture, give way to the lighter, more hopeful innocence and communal spirit of the children. Their pidgin-English speech, based on a miscellaneous cocktail of English dialect, North American pronunciation and staccato air-flight terms like Delta-Foxtrot-X-ray (which harks back to the time the aircraft crashed), is perhaps a little irritating at first but becomes a delight, as indeed do the children themselves with their sad and plaintive phrases like

'. . . their ain't no tomorrow-morrow land.'

Gibson's handsome features, enhanced at first with flowing, shoulder-length hair, then later with a more fashionable cropped style, added to his growing reputation as one of the modern screen's most natural action men. While often out-manoeuvred and vulnerable, sometimes confused and outplayed, he is always brilliantly, and optimistically, heroic, with those twinkling blue eyes and active, well-built body.

Thunderdome would become a major international success. But as the picture was being shot Gibson was miserable and uncooperative. George Miller remembered: 'He had the great burden of success on him. Acting for the screen was easy, he was a natural. But then, for no apparent reason, you've been anointed one of these demigod stars, when basically you think of yourself as an ordinary person just doing your job. It's a big conflict. Particularly with his Catholic upbringing.' According to Miller, by the third *Mad Max* picture his battle against this internal turmoil was strong. He was strained from overwork, but unable to halt the fast-moving conveyor belt of film-making that drained his strength and nervous energy.

Gibson explained his feelings more succinctly. 'I'd just done three films in a row and this was my fourth and I was going out of my mind.' He was also lacking the psychological boost of big success to sustain him. *Bounty*, with its thoughtful, but straightforward reconstruction of the historical facts, had seen Mel wrestle with a rather wimpish Fletcher Christian, an unhappy portrayal for a blossoming screen hero. *Mrs Soffel* likewise left him on unsteady ground. Only *The River*, perhaps, helped to refresh his downcast spirit.

But now he was drained of energy, motivation, ambition even. Still in his twenties, and with an impressive array of films, he found it increasingly hard to relax and keep a sense of proportion under pressure. 'At the end of the day I'd go out and get hammered, and then crawl into work next morning and do my thing,' he explained.

Doing his thing, on the set, was not the problem. In fact, some claimed it was a miracle that he remained totally professional when he was needed for a scene. But beyond the cameras it was obvious that he was moving close to the edge. It is said he virtually lost control of his drinking and would sometimes sink several beers before filming began. He was also smoking so much that his voice became affected. He tucked himself away when not on call for a scene. Long and tedious gaps in filming would be seen as an opportunity to grab another bottle and have yet another cigarette. His drinking prompted the producers to give him a round-the-clock service of car and driver.

The failure of his recent pictures to set the world on fire was making him tense and irritable. It was vital for his personal well-being that *Thunderdome* was a major success, and this placed him under further pressure. Little wonder that his temper and impatience was not improved when *People* magazine dubbed him 'the sexiest man alive'. It was a title he neither wanted, nor one he could escape from. Never naturally at ease with the press, Gibson became grudging and uncommunicative towards journalists visiting the set, even when he reluctantly agreed to talk to them. He was losing self-respect. He was unhappy with himself. But Miller claimed that his drinking never short-circuited his professionalism: he always turned up and was never drunk on the set.

One time, however, Miller did begin to chew his nails. 'Mel had stayed out one night and was late on the set,' he explained. 'I wondered if he had got into a fight or was lying injured somewhere. When he turned up I was angry, took him to one side and told him never to do that to me again.' A sequel to this incident brought forward a touch of the joky, irrepressible Mel of old, when he had to travel to an engagement in Melbourne and Miller reissued his warning. 'Don't worry, I'll be back in time,' assured Mel. Next morning he was seen running over the sand dunes dressed in a dinner jacket, bow tie and goggles, and carrying a glass and a bottle of champagne. As Miller explained: 'He staggered towards me pretending to be drunk, but then said, "Okay George, I'm ready for the first shot." ' Curiously, perhaps, it was Tina Turner who helped to nurse him back to reality. Genuinely concerned that he might be heading towards self-destruct, she sent him a photograph of himself, on the bottom of which she had written: 'Don't fuck this up.' During this dark period Gibson must have reflected on his earlier days in Sydney when he was an unknown, single young man, out for a good time. 'I was pretty wild in those days,' he once said. 'I'd get into a pub fight, generally trying to get someone else out of trouble.'

And he was an accomplished drinker. But his current situation was altogether darker.

It was the worst possible time for Gibson to be marooned in the dusty old mining town of Coober Pedy, where the picture was being made. Though only 500 miles (830 km) north-west of Adelaide (not too far by Australian standards), the location had been specially chosen for its bleak, barren-looking landscape. It can be very hot and very dry, with a wind that does nothing to freshen the atmosphere. It was tough and uncomfortable for everyone making the film, but ideal for the uncompromising moonscapes against which Mad Max would unravel his latest adventures. Amid soaring temperatures, heat exhaustion became a problem, tempers were stretched and Gibson was soon questioning his decision to make the picture. For this was no ordinary picture. It incorporated a phenomenal number of ambitious and physically punishing stunts.

Stunt actors did some of Mel's more dangerous scenes, which called for specialized skills, but among those he undertook himself was the 'big one'. It is the Thunderdome fight scene with Blaster, when each of them is harnessed into position at the end of a long elastic rope, the type used in bungy jumps. As they swing crazily back and forth, bouncing off the sides of the Thunderdome, they lash out at each other with lethal intent. 'Mel moved better than the stunt extras, so we decided to let him do the bumps and scrapes himself,' said Miller

Mad Max Beyond Thunderdome was released in the latter part of 1985 and immediately began to show its paces. Not all critics considered it the best of the trilogy and *Film Review*, assessing Gibson's career some years later, concluded that 'the story was not as compelling as the first two movies and Gibson did little to flesh out the central character'. On the other hand *Photoplay* commented: 'By adapting the story and populating it in abundance, Miller has made a Spielbergian version of his original concept which will undoubtedly turn Max from a cult hero into a superstar.' This review was bang on target, for the US box office alone would eventually top $40 million, three times the collective take from *The Bounty*, *Mrs Soffel* and *The River*.

It was some tangible consolation for Gibson, who continued to look back on the making of *Thunderdome* as one of the blackest periods of his career. He explained to one journalist: 'I didn't know at the time, but I was going around the twist. What I probably needed was some guys in white jackets.' Some of the later scenes were shot in the Melbourne area, but once the shutters had gone down on the hazardous four-month-long shoot, he wasted no time in returning to the sanity of Robyn and the children. He had promised himself a long and relaxing time away from the cameras once *Thunderdome* ended and he was as good as his word. Gradually the tensions eased. He played with his children, and for the first time really got to know William, his latest-born, who was now six months old. He rested more contentedly at night.

Reunited with his family at their beachside home at Coogee, mid-way between downtown Sydney and the historic Botany Bay, he resolutely fended off all movie offers. The pressures were off and he could swim in the sea and spend quality time with Robyn and his children. Those who have been closest to Mel over the years have talked about his devotion to his family, saying what a wonderful father he is. For Mel during this time, Coogee with his family was far more of a paradise than Tahiti without them.

It was during this domestic interlude at Coogee that Mel and Robyn looked around for their next house. Mel's spirits were rising, as were his confidence and self-esteem. Robyn and he had talked about buying a place in the country where they could have some cattle and horses, and which provided plenty of space for his growing family to move around freely. For the Gibsons had by no means given up on the idea of having more children.

Film-making was still very much on the back-burner when he and Robyn fell in love with a 6,000-acre farmstead set in beautiful Australian countryside close to Tangambalanga, in northern Victoria. They couldn't wait to move in and, once settled there, Mel continued his rehabilitation to normality. Days were by no means long and lazy. He worked hard on the farm, tending the cattle. Robyn said he even did his share of the domestic duties around the house. He had the chance to reunite with his mother and father when they arrived on long weekend visits. It was a time of taking stock, of reassessing what is of real value in life.

Gibson's self-imposed and much-enjoyed sabbatical lasted eighteen months. He renewed his confidence, regained his self-belief and emerged with a clearer and more balanced picture of life and his own priorities. He could even face being 'the sexiest man alive' with a detached and healthy degree of contempt. He admitted that in the darkest days he had thought seriously about giving up acting. But now he did not automatically put up the shutters when his agents called him from Sydney and Hollywood.

By mid 1986 Mel Gibson was ready to return to the business of making pictures. There was talk of a new drama set in Greece, possibly co-starring Australian actress Judy Davis, with Gillian Armstrong directing. Rumours were circulating about a possible James Bond project. And *The Running Man* (which he would eventually turn down after three years of speculation) was still said to be in the offing. But this time Mel Gibson was determined to write his own agenda.

9   Big-time Action Man

Tucking yourself away and out of sight just when you have made the most successful movie of your life could have signalled the end of Mel Gibson's career. Hollywood is not in the habit of tolerating rain checks. The place survives on change, new ideas, the latest fad and fashion. So Mel Gibson's not available - hey, who is Mel Gibson?

It says much for the talent and perceived potential of Gibson, even a decade or so ago, that he could change the rules. After an eighteen-month absence he returned with his appeal and popularity largely intact. Offers of work had never dried up, but he did not want to know. Once ready, he could have chosen from a shopping list of ideas. But Mel, though revitalized in spirit and body, was not interested in climbing back on to the Hollywood treadmill. Not straight away. So when someone suggested that he form his own production company, making pictures in Australia, it seemed like the ideal compromise. He would be back in business but able to make his own decisions about which pictures he would work on himself. It would also allow him to spend more time with Robyn and the children.

A reunion with noted Australian producer Pat Lovell, co-producer on *Gallipoli* had taken the idea a stage further and a partnership was formed in an atmosphere of optimism and promise. But despite the increasingly buoyant state of the Australian film industry, the plans did not work out. Suitable projects were hard to come by, and when they did, were always dependent on Gibson taking the starring role. It seemed to him to be just about the speediest possible climb back on to the very treadmill which he had found so painful to get off.

112

Meanwhile his American agent Ed Limato had been tapping into extremely positive vibes in Hollywood. Gibson was, indeed, well remembered and respected, not least by the top brass at Warner Brothers, basking in the financial success of *Thunderdome*. There were scores of possibilities, but the impact of *Mad Max* made him an automatic choice for some kind of 'action man' role. Not Arnie. Not Sly Stallone. He did not see himself in an unreal high voltage film world overrun by elaborate special effects. But he was drawn to a project about tough, committed cops in Los Angeles. *Lethal Weapon*, written by a 24-year-old newcomer to screenwriting, Shane Black, was concerned as much with exploring the relationship between two LA detectives as it was about sorting out crime. That is what appealed most strongly to Gibson, who headed off to Hollywood to talk about the project with director Richard Donner.

Donner's long career in the film business began in the late 1950s directing commercials. His two blockbusters on the big screen were *The Omen* (1976), a hugely successful devil movie starring Gregory Peck and Lee Remick, and *Superman* two years later, with Christopher Reeve and Marlon Brando. (Brando, incidentally, was said to have received $3 million for a ten-minute performance; and later had the effrontery to sue for a share of the gross!)

Once comfortably settled in Donner's Hollywood home it did not take Mel long to confirm his earlier instincts. *Lethal Weapon* was just the sort of project to tempt him back into the business. It seemed to have the right kind of realistic action and he was happy with the script and the choice of co-star. But the deal was not completely sealed, even after Mel and his proposed co-star, Danny Glover, read through a few lines of the script. Both had been recommended to Donner, who now needed to be convinced that they would be right, not only in their individual parts, but together. Within the delicate framework of their relationship, they needed to be able to generate the subtle humour that was inherent in the script.

In a sense they were an unlikely combination. Glover, the product of the Method school of acting, was serious, commanding, exact, undeviating. Gibson was more relaxed and flexible, more spontaneous and able to produce his best performances

113

'on the hoof'. Donner, not slow to pick up on the differences, finally made up his mind only after they had worked through more pages of script together. He was not being over-cautious - he knew the action sequences would not be a problem. However, the success of the picture would depend largely on the way the two cops were seen to react to each other. Indeed, their evolving relationship would emerge as the core of the movie. So Donner looked for the signs that would give him the confidence he needed. Gibson, for his part, later admitted that it took some time before the right chemistry took hold. 'But then we had real fun,' explained Mel. 'Danny's a great talent to bounce off.'

Glover, more than eight years Gibson's senior, was in his thirties before moving into films, first in a number of bit parts in the late 1970s and early 1980s. A serious, dignified actor, he had shown himself capable of handling delicate interpretations in the pivotal role of Moze, the farm worker, in Robert Benton's Oscar-winning *Places in the Heart* in 1984. A convincing performance in *The Color Purple* as Whoopi Goldberg's oppressive husband, and as a murderous cop in the Peter Weir-Harrison Ford hit, *Witness*, had confirmed him as a worthy candidate for Donner's new project. One aspect of his career which matched Gibson's was that he had moved into films after valuable experience in live theatre.

What no one could predict, neither Donner, Gibson, nor Glover, was the enormous success of the project on which they were about to embark. Among those reasonably confident about the outcome of *Lethal Weapon* was Joel Silver, who would co-produce alongside Richard Donner. In the 1980s Joel Silver emerged as Hollywood's leading producer of action-adventure movies, a reputation which gathered pace with the release of Arnold Schwarzenegger's *Commando* in 1985 and *Predator* two years later. It was a reputation comprehensively endorsed by the blockbuster response to the two *Lethal Weapon* movies released before the end of the decade.

The new film was a significant departure for Gibson. He had handled a wide range of roles in his six years of serious film-making, but *Lethal Weapon* would extend his range and bring him for the first time into the world of the mainstream police movie. Donner's selection would prove to be a telling piece of casting. As one authority would later explain: 'Gibson's reckless,

114

near-suicidal cop seemed to reflect his own intensity, love of language and goofy sense of humour.'

To help him to get under the skin of his character and the world he populates, Gibson went out on special assignments with the Los Angeles Police. He also did some hard martial arts training to prepare himself for the picture's combat sequences and went through a vigorous programme of weight-training to improve and toughen up his physique. Just as well, since much of the film is concerned with Mel's physical presence - not in shallow, exploitative terms, but legitimately in order to underpin the hardness of the man when, for instance, he is called upon to display his buttocks when getting out of bed, and then his chest as he is tortured with a live electrical cable.

Donner accepted that Gibson developed the character of Martin Riggs beyond the orbit of the script. Much of the success of the memorable scene when Riggs put the gun in his mouth came from Mel's own interpretation and handling. It was a difficult scene, potentially highly dangerous, even with the use of blank shots. But Gibson's commitment to it staggered even the experienced Donner. 'I couldn't believe what Mel was doing. It was so real I thought for a moment that he might have slipped a bullet into the gun. I stood frozen as Mel began to choke on the barrel and his finger pulled the trigger . . .' Mel, in choosing to extend the scene, had generated so much tension and realism that Donner sensibly kept the cameras running after the scheduled 'cut'.

Martin Riggs (Gibson) is a highly-strung cop and a sharpshooter whose capacity for survival has been honed on the killing fields of Vietnam. His wife has been killed in a car crash. Obsessive and manic, he is programmed to take risks. A move from narcotics to homicide is not a problem. The fact that they have given him Roger Murtaugh (Glover) as a partner most certainly is - for a start, he's 50 years old.

The picture plays hard from the start. Within a few minutes Riggs has almost blown his own head off. Then he jumps from the top of a building handcuffed to the man he is supposed to be talking out of a suicide attempt. Murtaugh wonders, Is this guy seriously mad, or just acting up as a way to get pensioned out of the force? In truth Riggs is suffering inside. After his wife's death, he is living on the edge and it is only his job that keeps

him going. An uneasy alliance is formed between the two partners as they begin to unravel the mystery of an apparent suicide
that turns out to be a murder . . . and much more. They are
brought closer together when Riggs saves his colleague's life.

To prepare them for their roles as cops both Gibson and
Glover trained for four weeks under the close scrutiny of stunt
coordinator, Mic Rogers. Donner said it was important that they
were able to move, act, react, talk and think the way cops do.
They had to be able to handle guns as if they had been doing it
all their lives. They needed to project an understanding of police
tactics. Rogers said that they fired off a thousand rounds of
blanks a day and were eventually able to handle all kinds of
firearms with great skill.

Gibson looks and plays the part. So does Glover. There are no
romantic attachments to get in the way. No sex. The nearest the
picture comes to suggesting any kind of relationship with a
woman is the photograph Riggs keeps of his dead wife. This
unusual absence prompted a flash of realization in the mind of
one critic, that despite his sexy image, 'Gibson's memorable
roles are not his romantic leads, but the hard-nosed loners.'
With no malice intended towards *Mad Max*, which had brought
him fame and a tidy fortune, Gibson honestly felt that his role
in *Lethal Weapon* was a significant step up, less restricted and
offering more scope for him to mould Martin Riggs in his own
vision. 'There was more opportunity for a wider interpretation,'
he said, and as he got more into the script he warmed to his
character.

Donner's careful casting paid off handsomely. Any doubts he
may have had about the ability of both actors to create that special relationship, so vital to the success of the movie, were swiftly swept aside. Nor need he have worried about Mel's tendency
to look deeply into his character and apply his own interpretation to the scenes he is playing. In fact it was much to Donner's
ultimate delight that Mel filled out the character of Martin Riggs
with great subtlety.

Among students of the genre *Lethal Weapon* won its creden-
tials as a convincing and honest all-action movie, if extremely
violent in parts. Moreover, it immediately hit the financial jack-
pot, taking an eye-opening $6.8 million during its first weekend
in the United States. After two weeks it led the US box office

with receipts of $20 million, going on to top $65 million. The worldwide take would soon reach more than $125 million.

Somehow, even during the making of the picture, everyone seemed convinced that *Lethal Weapon* was destined to be a winner. Indeed a second *Lethal Weapon* was already in the planning stages when the final scenes of the original were being shot. Richard Donner, in his determination to direct *Lethal Weapon 2*, readily broke the habit of a lifetime, never to make a sequel.

Gibson could not have wished for a more devastatingly successful return to filming. The bonus was that he really enjoyed working on it. He was refreshed and renewed from his lay-off. He had the energy and the deep, attentive interest which had been sucked out of him by the incessant bombardment of his earlier crippling schedule. Adding to his joy was the nearness of Robyn and his children. The whole family had settled into a rented house in Beverly Hills within days of his signing the contract.

Mel was frank about his eighteen months 'drop out'. He told the press that it gave him time to reflect and to relax. 'Becoming a movie star isn't the easiest thing in the world to handle,' he explained. 'One day you can walk down the street and nobody notices you. Then all that changes and it can all get out of hand.' Mel admitted at this point that his doctor had warned him about the condition of his liver. 'I decided it was time to quit drinking,' he said.

But planned or not, a second *Lethal Weapon* would have to wait a while. Mel was already down to do *Tequila Sunrise* with Michelle Pfeiffer and Kurt Russell. He and agent Limato had chosen this project because it would enable Gibson to develop a completely different role from that of Riggs in *Lethal Weapon* especially since his return as Riggs was already virtually assured. Another attraction was that it would be filmed in Hollywood, which meant Mel would continue to be close to his wife and family on an almost daily basis.

Tequila Sunrise plunged Mel into the world of drugs, playing cocaine dealer Dale McKussic. When planning what he says will be his final drugs run, McKussic clashes with an old friend from high school, Nick Frescia, played by Russell, who is now heading the Los Angeles narcotics squad. Further complications arise when both become romantically involved with beautiful restau-

117

rant owner Jo Ann Vallenari (Michelle Pfeiffer). The picture ultimately focuses on the need of all three to make fundamental and potentially painful choices. Dale has to choose between life inside or outside the law. Nick must decide between personal and professional obligations. Jo Ann realizes she cannot have both Dale and Nick.

Mel surprised just about everyone by signing to do the movie. He had always claimed he would not consider a role which linked him to drugs use. Only a few years before, in greater financial need than now, he had flatly turned down the lead in an Australian movie called *Monkey Grip* for no other reason than that he would have had to play a drug addict. Yet this was a project from Patricia Lovell, his long-term friend and respected colleague. Surely she, if anyone, could have persuaded Mel to think again. After all it was a good script.

Against this background Mel was never totally convincing in his explanation for doing *Tequila Sunrise* and was awkward and uneasy under questioning. The script had already spawned one dilemma. Harrison Ford had agreed to do the part before Gibson, but pulled out within twenty-four hours because he, too, was worried about the ramifications of playing a drug dealer.

The director of *Tequila Sunrise* was the well-respected Robert Towne, a celebrated screenwriter with an even greater reputation in his earlier career as a script-doctor, rewriting basically good ideas and bringing them commercially up to standard. He made an impressive directorial debut with *Personal Best* in 1982, a fine character study of a lesbian athlete, which he had also written and which was backed by Warner Brothers. Gibson was not alone in his admiration of Towne, who had been involved in the 1970s in such compelling offerings as *Chinatown* in 1974 and *Shampoo* a year later. He had also written *Tequila Sunrise*, but this time Warners, who were to finance the creative development work on the film, dragged their feet, also uneasy about the idea of the hero being a drug dealer. Towne refused to rewrite his material to avoid this sticking point and the project hung around for a long time without finding a home. Warners finally offered their finance on the proviso of a big name agreeing to star in the key role. They had been well satisfied with Ford, but withdrew again when he walked away.

Mel Gibson's signature not only brought the project back to life, but enabled Ed Limato to draft into the scheme of things a new and highly promising client named Michelle Pfeiffer, whose alluring beauty and talent had first been spotted in *Grease 2* (1982). In a sense *Tequila Sunrise* had a hard job following *Lethal Weapon*. Two enormous blockbusters in a row was surely too much to expect, but Towne's skills and reputation as a director virtually guaranteed a picture of substance and quality. For some critics the formula of the picture, old-world romance blended with an ample dose of suspense and melodrama, was rather dated. Even Towne may have implied some kind of self-doubt on this point when he later said simply that 'Mel made the movie work.' But for his part, Gibson had taken to the script from the start, even though he felt the story became over-involved and unfolded sluggishly.

Gibson's Dale McKussic is a half-reformed drug trafficker who says he wants to give up the business. But at the same time he chooses to help a relative with a cocaine deal and, on a much larger scale, repays an old debt by aiding Mexico's most notorious drugs smuggler with a multi-million dollar accounting fraud. Pitted against him stands Russell's Nick Frescia, a cop who has recently been promoted to help the local drugs squad. His impact has as yet been marginal. As Frescia and McKussic are old high school buddies, they drift into a live-and-let-live kind of relationship. But this is under threat when anti-drugs agents concoct a scam to put Gibson behind bars and Russell is drafted to assist.

Tequila Sunrise would be remembered for the delicate balances and precise interpretations achieved by the main players, rather than the strength and significance of its storyline. Gibson's performance was widely praised, some critics claiming it represented his best work to that date. And Pfeiffer proved she could act with a superb delicacy. Their love scenes together highlighted a surprising and up to this point neglected aspect of Mel's performances. But he showed he was equal to the demands, his kitchen table scene with Pfeiffer being described by one critic as 'deliciously romantic and delicately erotic'; the same writer claimed that their hot tub scene 'redefines the word steamy . . . though it is all real romance, love the way it ought to be.'

119

In the end *Tequila Sunrise* did no one involved any harm and enjoyed a good, if not ecstatic, public response, grossing almost $30 million through the US box office. That was good enough for Mel, who had been well pleased with the $1.5 million fee Ed Limato had negotiated on his behalf. And in any event he was soon fully concentrated on his next project, his most lucrative yet.

While Mel and his family snatched some time together, resting and relaxing back in Australia between this latest crop of pictures, events had been leading to the inevitable sequel to *Lethal Weapon*. And at Warner Brothers they were still talking about the 45,000 fan letters addressed to Mel Gibson which had piled up in just three weeks after the release of the first in the series. By the time Mel returned with Robyn and the children to his Hollywood base, most of the familiar elements from the first offering were back in position. Richard Donner was once again directing. He and Joel Silver were the producers. The production was in the hands of Silver Pictures and the movie would be released through Warners. Danny Glover was there again, alongside Gibson, and the cast had been given an additional dimension through British stars Joss Ackland, playing the villainous South African Diplomat, Arjen Rudd, and London-born Patsy Kensit, who plays his innocent assistant, Rika Van Den Haas. Patsy, though only twenty-one, was already a movie veteran. She made her film début at the age of four as Mia Farrow's daughter in *The Great Gatsby*. Also added to the cast was Joe Pesci, best known for his portrayal of Jake La Motta's brother in Martin Scorsese's *Raging Bull* in 1980. He plays Leo Getz, a troublesome, thrill-seeking, would-be police officer.

The follow-up is a legitimate sequel with a credible development of relationships and themes established in the first *Lethal Weapon*. The most important of these is how Martin Riggs (Gibson) is now getting along with his partner against crime, Roger Murtaugh (Glover). And the excellent script, this time penned by Jeffrey Boam from a story by Shane Black and Warren Murphy, succeeds handsomely in doing just that, both by developing a mutual understanding between the two partners and from observing the natural changes in each of them that time has brought about.

As Gibson explained at the time: 'When we first met Riggs in

Lethal Weapon we found him at one of his lowest points. Now, because of the events of that film, he has gotten over his personal hurdles and is not harbouring the same kind of hostilities towards himself.' Certainly, the once-suicidal Riggs has mellowed, but Glover's character has also been cleverly advanced. He is less sensitive to provocation and has more inner confidence in the relationship. What is impressive is the subtlety of the development – essential since they are both the same people, still with their individual instincts. This restraint is perhaps most detectable when the duo are tipped off about the location of a major drugs ring headquarters. Murtaugh wants to pause and think about it for a moment, but Riggs is already half-way through the door shouting his rhyming couplets over his shoulder. Riggs remains full of adrenalin and still lives the only way he knows how, close to the edge. But the difference in Riggs from the original *Lethal Weapon*, as Richard Donner explained, 'is that now he stops to figure out the odds, because he wants to live.'

That change made way for the introduction of a further key element, that of humour – not belly-laughs, much quieter, gentler. Often it's almost subliminal, as when the long-suffering Murtaugh casts a knowing glance in Riggs's direction. It is also there through a relaxation of the deep tensions that often surfaced between them in the earlier film. Riggs is now less manically exuberant. In the tip-off scene (above) Murtaugh insists on calling the station. Riggs prefers action, springing to life and ready to go off in pursuit. 'C'mon, Rog . . .', he pleads with his partner, 'Don't be a killjoy. We're back! We're bad! You're black! I'm mad! This is gonna be great.'

The easier relationship is not surprising. After all, they've now been riding around in the same car for three years. 'They're almost like a married couple,' commented Gibson. 'They still argue and bicker, but now it's over inconsequential things, like who gets the pastrami on rye.'

Lethal Weapon 2 is an explosive sequel and starts when Riggs and Murtaugh are assigned to provide protective custody for accountant Leo Getz (Joe Pesci), who has used his creative talents to launder nearly half a billion dollars in illicit narcotics money. It is a routine, uneventful duty they find boring until, that is, they discover that the laundered money has come from the very syndicate they have been seeking to smash for years. That syndicate wants Leo dead and their chief 'enforcer', Pieter Vorstedt (Derrick O'Connor), has no inhibitions about killing anyone who might get in the way, including, if necessary, a couple of cops in a police car. Leo's information leads Riggs and Murtaugh directly to the head of the syndicate, the icy Arjen Rudd (Joss Ackland), a protected South African diplomat to the United States.

This only sharpens the interest and resolve of Riggs and Murtaugh. Now they are really interested – to hell with diplomatic immunity. When Riggs gets mad, even the impossible arrest becomes possible. The detectives' unexpected arrival shocks not only Rudd, but also his beautiful assistant, Rika Van Den Haas (Patsy Kensit). While Rika has never had any reason to question her employer's activities, her introduction to Riggs and Murtaugh leaves her with some serious doubts, and she begins to question her allegiances. By this time Martin Riggs's interest in Rika appears to be stretching far beyond the call of duty. The plot moves into a darker mood when Riggs discovers that the ruthless Pieter Vorstedt was responsible for the death of his wife and, drama upon drama, will go on to kill his new girl-friend after their first date. With most of Murtaugh's department killed, and Riggs himself seriously injured, the drug syndicate is finally smashed.

The big-scale action sequences are more spectacular than in the earlier picture. Donner maintained this came about not from cynical manipulation, but rather through the natural evolution of the plot and characters. 'A lot of films are written for special effects and stunts, and then the characters are made to fit the action,' explained Donner. 'When we made the first *Lethal Weapon* we concentrated on the characters and, out of the insanity of the characters, evolved the action pieces. The same thing happened in *Lethal 2*. As the characters evolved further, so did the situations they were thrown into.'

Fans of the original *Weapon* were certainly not to be disappointed by the fast and furious action sequences. There is the high-speed car chase, in which two detectives in an unmarked police car, with a dozen more vehicles behind, weave crazily in and out of traffic in pursuit of a red BMW. Then suddenly a shotgun blast shatters the windscreen of the law car. But the most ambitious set-piece entailed the complete destruction of a Hollywood Hills house on stilts with Gibson and Glover standing very close by, a scene considered crucial to the picture. When Richard Donner first read the scene in the script he just could not see how it could be done. 'I sat with Joel Silver, production designer Michael Riva and special effects coordinator Matt Sweeney over a period of months trying to think of an effective way to put it on film,' he explained. Often such scenes are done in miniature, but Donner ruled it out. 'The scene needs a sense of reality and it needs the actors to be there as it happens,' he concluded.

In the end, two separate duplicates of the house were constructed. The first was built on Stage 1 of the Burbank Studios, where a system of hydraulics enabled Donner to film the trembling and rocking house with the actors inside, before the 10-ton structure collapsed on the stage floor. The other duplicate was built in Newhall, twenty miles north of Los Angeles. 'You could actually live in this house,' said Michael Riva. 'That was because the local authorities would not let crew members work inside the house unless it was structurally sound.' For the same reason the foundations, on caissons and steel, were driven thirty-five feet into the earth. Gibson, Glover and Pesci were strategically placed in the scene, but in a safe position. When Donner finally gave the signal, nine separate cameras filmed the drama as the house crashed down to the bottom of the hill.

In contrast to the ambitious and complicated nature of the action sequences was the simple effectiveness of some of the film's most humorous moments. One of the more amusing takes place in the home of Murtaugh, who is seen firmly rooted to the toilet seat because it has been wired to explode when he stands up (said to be Mel's idea). After Glover has been marooned on the loo seat for some time, they agree: a count of three and Mel will haul him off, the pair then hurling themselves sideways to avoid the blast. The end of the film prompted a vintage ad lib. Donner had given Mel cautious licence to improvise if his experience and instincts as an actor suggested it. There is an almighty shoot-out and when the dust settles and with sirens indicating the arrival of the police, we find a badly injured Mel with Glover, their faces close together. Says Mel (not in the script), 'Come on . . . give us a kiss before they come.'

123

But some other aspects fared less well with the critics. The picture ran into allegations of being excessively bloody. With some justification for there were, after all, some thirty fatalities – by shooting, explosion, decapitation and by Mel's bare hands. One scene was said to use baddies as a 'cheap target for jingoism thinly disguised as socio-political statement-making.' Another is singled out because it interprets the Riggs line, 'Tonight I'm not a cop – this is personal,' as less a form of token revenge, more a vigilante call – one which, significantly, is never questioned in the script. Still, as the same writer pointed out, 'It is after all, just a movie. So if you like your action fast, your humour coarse and you respond to lines like "We're back! We're bad! You're black! I'm mad!" then this one is for you.'

It must have been 'the one' for many, for the US box office alone – at $147 million – was more than double the equivalent take for the first *Lethal Weapon*. It even stood its ground against such recognized blockbuster competition as a new *Indiana Jones* movie, the latest *James Bond* and *Batman*.

Towards the end of filming Mel had expressed his anxieties about doing a sequel. 'Notoriously, they're never as good as the original, and you feel a lot of pressure to live up to the standards that you've already set,' he explained. 'The reason we've done this film is that we liked the characters and saw an opportunity to take them up another avenue and have some more fun. I think we've managed to do that successfully, because I had a great time and I think the audience will too.'

They certainly did. For Gibson, *Lethal Weapon 2* was so far easily the biggest success of his career.

10 More than Just the Movies

Near constant filming, devotion to a wife and growing family, handling his celebrity status, planning his financial future and, when forced into it, talking to journalists and giving media interviews has left little time to spare in Mel Gibson's life.

Or so you would think. But over the years the wise-cracking Mel has somehow found time to direct the serious side of his nature towards a number of issues he considers crucial, important, or just plain wrong, including nuclear testing, the privacy of his wife and family, sexual 'deviations' and even politics. His motivation is often deep-seated and probably originates in the strong behavioural and moral codes which Hutton and Anne Gibson handed down to their children.

Even today Mel will tell you that his father is his personal hero, always has been and always will be. 'I learned from him that you should never quit and never stop striving to improve yourself,' he once said. His Catholic beliefs are similarly abiding and deep-rooted. It is no secret that he is against abortion, birth control, feminism and homosexuality. And when he looks back into the history of Ireland, significant because of his family roots, the bitter violence and high emotive issues of the battles of the Black and Tans in 1920-21 could arguably have left faded scars on his psyche. More than one observer hinted, though Gibson might well deny it, that it was his subliminal feelings that drew him instinctively to the story of Scotland's fight for independence in *Braveheart*. This led to some claims that the film was obliquely political, i.e. anti-British.

When Gibson brushed with politics in 1987 he was not exact-ly trail-blazing. Several of Hollywood's traditional 'greats' over the years had indulged in positive campaigning. Contemporary artists like Barbra Streisand, Warren Beatty, Jane Fonda, Arnold Schwarzenegger and Frank Sinatra did not hesitate to declare openly their convictions at one time or another. Clint Eastwood even became mayor of Carmel, while Reagan made the supreme jump from Hollywood to the White House.

Gibson's involvement was small-time by comparison, helping the 27-year-old Australian truck-driver and fellow Catholic, Robert Taylor, in the run-up to Australia's Federal election. Even then it was ostensibly a behind-the-scenes role, though his motives were strong and his intent sincere. For Taylor was artic-ulating many of the principles which Mel held dear. He was against the trend towards the liberalization of many aspects of Australian life. He was against the growing domination of big business, higher taxation, the new welfare culture, which per-mitted, even encouraged, an increasing number of work-shy, irresponsible individuals and drop-outs to claim financial hand-outs. Some ten years later, when he was awarded the highest honour in Australia for service to the country, the Order of Australia, he continued to condemn the politics of the earlier Prime Minister, Bob Hawke, and his successor Paul Keating. In 1987 Gibson considered Taylor sincere enough, but thought his campaigning rhetoric lacked the sharp edge and inspiration nec-essary to get himself elected. He needed a harder message, one which concentrated minds and raised important doubts, even fears. Mel used the interval between films to put his shoulder behind Taylor's campaign. He drove his campaign truck from place to place. He rewrote some of his speeches. With Mel's help Taylor was now talking about falling values, the steep decline into drug abuse, paedophilia and pornography. Mel's presence brought in the crowds. As one report observed: 'When Mel applauded, they all applauded.'

Their first meeting had taken place in the living room of Mel's Sydney home and at that time it is doubtful if Gibson felt confident that he could make much difference to Taylor's cam-paign. He certainly wanted to, since his current disillusionment was the result of years of increasing frustration with the way he saw politics developing in Australia.

Taylor's approach lacked presentation skills, Gibson considered. He needed to talk to journalists in short catchphrases, using words and ideas that would make headlines. He needed to create a greater impact when addressing public meetings. But as an independent candidate Taylor had little realistic chance of winning against his more powerful opponents. As the Taylor-Gibson bandwagon moved around from place to place, it was not clear if the voters had simply turned out to see Mel or to hear Taylor, despite Gibson doing all he could to stay in the background.

In the end Taylor did better than expected and Gibson left that particular political trail to return to Hollywood, somewhat chastened perhaps, but not in the least regretful. As he told a journalist when referring to his children having been born in Australia: 'I can't think of anything more challenging or important than making sure we can guarantee the future for our young ones.'

Five years later he was still concerned about a changing world and the part being played by modern politics. He told a reporter: 'I've gotten more involved in politics lately. Seeing it for what it really is, you get these frustrations when you read the newspapers and see what a circus we're in. At times I feel like chucking the towel in, pulling up roots and going to some island somewhere. But then you realize that you must never abandon hope.'

Over the years his strong, traditional principles have often made him feel at odds with modern life, despite his outgoing professional image and he has been an intermittent target for gay and lesbian groups. In 1990 his fleeting portrayal of a hairdresser in *Bird on a Wire* was criticised as 'demeaning' and he was singled out again three years later in his directorial début, *The Man Without a Face*. His character in the book on which the picture was based was a gay teacher involved with a fourteen-year-old student. The script changed this to a heterosexual teacher wrongly accused of molesting a child. This brought Gibson under the hammer, though the record shows that the changes had been made before he signed to do the picture.

When confronted with a situation, he has resolutely defended his uncompromising attitude concerning sex, though he is not normally combative or even assertive. He makes no excuses for

127

holding strict and traditional views, despite opponents' allegations that he is homophobic and living in the dark ages. When occasionally he has been drawn to comment his response is barely repeatable. *Braveheart* brought him under fire yet again. He faced claims that he had turned Edward into a 'typical homophobic caricature.'

It is unlikely that Gibson would lose too much sleep over these accusations, though he was probably realistic enough to recognize the potential ill-will that can result from acquiring any kind of 'anti' reputation – especially the 'anti-gay' tag in Hollywood. He certainly demonstrated courage when he accepted an invitation to attend a seminar run by the Gay and Lesbian Alliance against Defamation, a media watchdog group that had repeatedly spoken out about what they felt to be his homophobic views. His attempt to build bridges came after the powerful gay community began boycotting his films.

In 1995 the French nuclear tests in the Pacific was another 'anti' issue about which Gibson felt strongly enough to make his feelings public. He had been awarded the prestigious *Chevalier des Arts et Lettres* by the French government, but he refused to turn up to receive the award as a demonstration of his disapproval. At the European launch of *Braveheart* he received a standing ovation from an audience of 2,000 when he denounced the tests during a speech at the Venice Film Festival. 'I wish they wouldn't do it. I have family there. I love Australia,' he said. The French had insisted on going ahead with their test programme in the French Polynesian Pacific despite strong and persistent protests and boycotts in his native Australia, where the tests were seen, moral issues apart, as being far too close for comfort. Official sources explained away Gibson's absence by claiming he was fully committed to a busy programme of promotion for *Braveheart*, but Gibson himself brought the truth out into the open. 'It was a definite decision to make a protest against the nuclear testing,' he said.

Gibson has also fought strongly for his own privacy and for the right, when not on official film business, to be left to lead an unencumbered and uninvaded personal life. His early years as a major star were noteworthy for his efforts to keep his private life private, and he reacted angrily when books and press features gave graphic accounts of his so-called adventures. He has most stubbornly of all, and with not a little moral courage because it would often have been easier to give in to the pressures, repelled attempts to involve his wife and family in any kind of media exposure.

Through the years Robyn has fiercely maintained a low profile but, according to a *Braveheart* crew member, she is clearly the most powerful and important figure in Gibson's life. Said to have a keen sense of humour and a ready wit, the 5 foot 6 inch Mrs Gibson has dark brown hair, a flashing smile and, even as the children begin to grow up, still considers herself a full-time mother. The way she and Mel have hauled their kids around on location has brought out some critics, but Mel maintains it has helped them to expand their horizons and given them a good, cosmopolitan education. Where possible, they are generally enrolled in the nearest school rather than have a tutor conduct their education in the home.

Robyn has been central to his life and career and was enormously supportive when he finally did something about his drinking. But Mel hedges when asked how he proposed to her. 'Clumsily . . .' he faltered, though he did once reveal that he and Robyn made a pact on their wedding night that they would stay together for the rest of their lives. Over the years he has certainly done a good job in enabling Robyn and the children to have as normal a life as possible in the circumstances, one outside the public gaze. This commitment to shield them is simply a reflection of what he believes – that everyone has a right to privacy. It is just one among the values imparted to him as a child.

Being so focused on his marriage cuts little ice with the more hard-nosed sections of the media. Mel knows the score. 'I think many people are irritated by my image as a good husband,' he once said. But in more recent years Gibson himself has become more relaxed, more tolerant and more resigned to living with the pressures of being an international mega-star in an era when the press is all-pervasive. Director George Miller said: 'It took him many years to come to terms with all this, but he has done it gracefully. He has learned not to take it too seriously and to be sustained by his work.' Robyn has shown outstanding strength, remaining resolutely behind the scenes and taking care of their six children. 'His wife is a great levelling influence,' explained Miller.

Gibson is only too well aware that his work takes him from his wife and family far too often and for too long a time. Commonly, he takes to joking about it, but his feelings are deep and sincere. Even when shooting in a 'home' studio, the long days mean he does not see his kids as often as he would like. Nearing the end of shooting on *Conspiracy Theory*, he told a writer for *Vanity Fair* that he was looking forward to getting them all in one room and standing them up and then slowly going around, one by one, shaking their hands and saying: 'Hi, I'm your dad.'

A bizarre incident which seriously disturbed Gibson took place during a heavy storm in Sydney when he suddenly found a strange woman peering in through one of the windows of his house. Explained Gibson: 'It was like a horror movie. I went to the back of the house and the windows were closed and I looked out and she was staring right through.' He told her to go home and went upstairs to bed. But the incident didn't end there and she was later found balancing herself on the roof. The police were called but she disappeared before they arrived, leaving messages scrawled across the windows in lipstick.

Defending the right of his wife and family to have a private life is probably Mel Gibson's greatest, certainly his most constant, crusade of all.

11   From Comedy . . .

Lethal Weapon 2 was released in 1989. Early that year, on 3 January, Mel Gibson celebrated his thirty-third birthday. Much had changed since 1978 and *Summer City*. He had now made fourteen movies. He had become a star with *Mad Max*, and two blockbusting *Lethal Weapon*s had transformed him into a megastar. His income in basic fees alone was now counted in millions of dollars.

But he was still the same old Mel. Or was he? Life and circumstances had made their demands. The Mel Gibson whose identity had been firmly Australian in those early years was now, inevitably, making his big money in America, the country of his birth. Hollywood had become such an integral part of his and his family's future, that before starting work on *Lethal Weapon 2* he had bought a home there.

His luxurious new property was in California's exclusive Sierra Canyon in Malibu, splendidly located just a mile or so from the coast. He bought it from rock singer Rick Springfield in 1989. But even at this stage in his career he already owned three other properties. He had purchased his first beach house in Coogee, near Sydney, in 1983 and a year later added a more modest, yet luxuriously appointed three-bedroom apartment in California's fashionable Santa Monica.

In 1985, to escape from personal intrusion after making *Mad Max 2*, he bought his 6,000 acre cattle ranch farm at Tangambalanga, in the picturesque Kiewa Valley in northern Victoria, mid-way between Sydney and Melbourne. It was here that Mel would take every opportunity to relax in the saddle and repair after the ravages of near-constant film-making.

At first his Kiewa Valley property was simply a sanctuary where he could put his feet up and let the days drift by. As time went on he became seriously interested in cattle breeding. In the Kiewa Valley Mel Gibson was never the famous movie-star slumming it for a week or two in a palatial property masquerading as a farm. No high-wire security fence signalled his privacy to anyone who might feel inclined to invade it. 'You can't live your life that way,' he once told a surprised journalist. By this time he was having to live his life under the burden of being dubbed 'the sexiest man alive'. But that did not prevent him from mingling with local people as one of them, an ordinary cattle-farm owner who might never have been near a movie camera for all they cared.

His celebrity status never hindered life on the farm. As the need or mood dictated, he would drive his station wagon into the nearby town of Tangambalanga. The locals recognized him as Mel Gibson, of course, but that was all. They would chat to him about farming and horses, whether the much-needed rain would materialize that day and other routine issues concerning their lives in the valley.

This impressive spread, along with his other properties, amounted to a substantial portfolio which Mel would augment over the years. He bought his 13,500-acre Beartooth ranch in Montana, where he breeds cattle, in the same year (1989) he took over Springfield's former home, and in 1990 purchased two further Australian properties, along with some land. The most expensive was an 8,900-acre farm at Limerick Springs, little more than a stone's throw from his Tangambalanga spread. He then bought 4,350 acres of rough hill country at Bullioh, in the nearby upper Murray region. His second property purchase that year, also in the state of Victoria, was a luxury hotel in Yackandandah, which Robyn secured at auction with the intention of having it restored and transformed into a profitable business.

In 1992, the year in which the third *Lethal Weapon* would be released, he bought a beach house less than four miles from his other home in Malibu. Carefully situated in the superstar belt, this magnificent property has a long stretch of private beach where Mel and his family can relax in total privacy. He is said to use a golf buggy when he wants to go down to the water's edge.

Mel's house collecting seems to verge on the obsessional,

though his motives are not altogether clear. One view is that having come up the hard way, he needs some tangible evidence to show he has made it to the top. But the estate agents have certainly been kept busy. Since 1992 Gibson has purchased yet another house, this time in Greenwich, Connecticut, close to his place of birth on the East Coast. And he was rumoured to be eyeing some rather splendid apartments in New York. After finishing *Braveheart* in 1995 he began thinking seriously about buying a property in Scotland. More rumours have recently filtered through about a place in Alaska, far away from the Hollywood spotlight.

His spending on property and land is undoubtedly a sound investment for the future. Meanwhile, having his own places is important for family reasons. With houses close to areas of filming, Robyn and the children are never too far away when he is working.

Love for his family has been Gibson's deepest on-going obsession. Robyn and the children are central to his existence. He is devoted to them. Over the years occasional reports of fleeting liaisons and 'indiscretions' have now and then bubbled to the surface. His obvious physical appeal and spirited behaviour have sometimes brought him press attention he would rather have done without. But nothing even remotely begins to challenge the special relationship which Gibson has with his wife and family.

During his days of struggle in Australia, through his mediocre years, on through the success of *Mad Max* and then the superstardom that came with *Lethal Weapon*, the family provided a deep purpose to everything he did, giving a shape, balance and perspective to his life. This strong sense of kinship, along with his and their spiritual belief, has been the very basis of his life, not simply as a film actor, but as a private being as well. He has been photographed, Bible in hand, walking to church with his children. When film commitments allow he regularly attends Sunday mass at the Chapel of the Canyons in a remote region of San Fernando Valley, Los Angeles.

But Mel does not go in for parading his family. Nor does he declare his Roman Catholicism from the rooftops. But he does not deliberately hide it away either. Like his father Hutton, whom he loves and respects and continues to see as an example to follow, he is committed to the faith. But it is something deeply within him. He does not feel that it needs to be articulated all the time. He will seldom, if ever, bring up the subject as a topic of conversation. He regards his faith as very private and of no concern to others.

Family, sex, religion – what have they to do with his status as a film actor? When a journalist asked him about his spiritual life, he hesitated, then talked reluctantly and rather awkwardly: 'Oh no . . . we're not getting into this?' Pressed further, his views were simple, humble almost. 'Well . . . I mean, you have only one life; stands to reason there's more on the other side, and that how one conducts oneself here is somehow related to it.' When asked if he followed the ways of the Church, he responded seriously enough, though, typically, avoided divulging any of his deep beliefs to a journalist. 'I try,' he said, 'but I'm not saying that I am a complete all-the-time success.'

But then Mel Gibson seldom wants to get heavy about anything. On personal matters his answers are typically evasive. He likes to keep things light, whether on a film set, scrambling around with his kids or working on the farm. Having fun is his recipe for survival in the picture-making business. He loves his practical jokes and silly pranks. Mel will always be the one wearing the funny hat. Or in a pub he'll be the clown balancing a pint on his forehead. *Lethal Weapon* director Richard Donner suggests he sometimes fools around as a means of keeping his distance, as a defensive technique. 'Gibson has little interest in baring his soul,' he explained. Then added: 'But really, he's a big, sweet, loveable, honest kid.' American journalist Bart Mills, out to catch the serious side of the elusive star, said Gibson uses humour to deflect anyone seeking to probe the personality behind the performance.

He is something of a hybrid. He can be shy and withdrawn, yet often when working on a picture he will be relaxed and friendly on the set, enjoying moving around and talking to people rather than tucking himself away until his scenes come along.

But he does have his genuinely serious moments, often when he is talking about Robyn and his children.

My wife and my family are my sanity. Robyn was a real help to me when I first got successful and it did sort of go to my head. It was Robyn who was strong enough to separate herself from my fame and

success. Robyn was able to keep my feet on the ground. She doesn't
see me as a sex symbol. She hasn't got my picture stuck up on the
wall. She leaves notes for me, like, 'Do the dishes'.

But back as the funny man, Mel jokes: 'I call Robyn my Rock
of Gibraltar, only she's prettier.' And about his children? 'Sure,
they live in the attic at home. They're very easy to keep – I give
them puppy food and take them out for a walk once a day in the
park!' On a good day he is irrepressible.

And so is his film career. The moment he finished work on
Lethal Weapon 2, he left California for Canada, to work on a
comedy with Goldie Hawn. The picture would fulfil two of his
long-held ambitions. A year or two later Gibson would publicly
reveal, perhaps not all that seriously, that the talent of the stand-
up comedian is one he would most like to have. His role in *Bird
on a Wire*, while not that of a stand-up comic, nonetheless took
him for the first time into the serious business of comedy, which
he had long yearned to do. The other ambition was to work with
the effervescent Goldie Hawn.

Two important aspects of Gibson's attitude to his career surfaced at about this time. Almost from the beginning, with the
occasional exception, he had thought carefully about the projects pitched to him. Ed Limato's recommendations, however
astute and wisely considered, did not always prevail. Gibson
passed over many movies which did major business at the box
office or were critically acclaimed. Michael Keaton stepped in as
Batman after Gibson turned it down. His rejection of Robin
Hood left the way wide open for Kevin Costner. *Final Analysis*
fell to Richard Gere after Gibson turned the other way. And he
gave the thumbs-down to *Champions* and more significantly,
Days of Thunder, a big hit for Tom Cruise.

Many ideas were ruled out, first, because he was wary of
being typecast. Others because he simply did not take to them or
they would separate him from the security of his family. His
decisions were mostly based on instinct. It said much for his reputation in the early 1990s that he could pick and choose to the
extent he did yet still have a highly lucrative work schedule
stretching well into the future. It was not always easy for him to
control the instinctive demands of the work ethic, and he soon
found himself again sailing close to the wind of mental and phys-

ical stress as one project quickly followed the last; sometimes they even overlapped. *Bird on a Wire* (for a fee of $3.5 million) and *Air America* ($4.2 million) were both released in 1990 and were quickly followed in 1991 by *Hamlet*, for which Gibson was happy to accept just $700,000.

He had first met Goldie Hawn on the set of *Tequila Sunrise* when she visited his co-star, Kurt Russell, with whom she was then living. They all became good friends. Hawn hadn't done a picture for some time and Gibson was anxious to do a comedy. When *Bird on a Wire* came along it suited both of them. The picture found little favour among the critics, nor did it score heavily financially, when set against the impact of the *Lethal Weapon* movies. All the same, $65 million through the US box office made it the joint second highest earner, along with *Lethal Weapon 1* of all Gibson's pictures to that time. (*Lethal Weapon 2* came top.)

Bird on a Wire was ridiculous slapstick with a banal script, but it was also gloriously outrageous and uproariously funny. It was essentially a hyperactive chase movie with improbable incident mounting on improbable incident. The changing scene takes in motor cars, motor cycles, an airplane and a scary roller-coaster ride. The zoo sequences towards the end stretch one's credulity to breaking point, even for the most diehard Gibson and Hawn fans. However, Mel's eyes have never twinkled more brightly, nor has Goldie's smile been wider. Against the frenetic backdrop, an old-fashioned romance develops. The story goes that, unbeknown to director John Badham, the two co-stars conspired to tone down the picture's sole important love scene via secret late-night telephone calls. In the context of the movie, Goldie later declared that the original scene would have been a turn-off. 'It just wasn't right to see these two people go at it together.' She was probably right. The lovemaking, as seen by the paying public, has the co-stars in bed together in a motel room, but the scene is simply funny. Similarly, it is laughter the film-makers go for when Gibson takes down his pants to have pellets removed from his backside. This was a form of self-revelation fast becoming a habit. For this was the third time that a movie had scripted Mel Gibson with his rear-end showing, from *Gallipoli* to *Lethal Weapon* and now to *Bird on a Wire*, with *Forever Young* yet to come! Not forgetting of course, that celebrated 'off-screen' viewing during the making of *Summer City*. And Mel was worried about being typecast . . .?

The film has a simple plot. Rick (Gibson) is in serious trouble. He has been in hiding ever since he turned state's witness against the sort of baddies you simply do not cross. Marianne (Hawn) becomes involved when she pulls up for petrol and discovers her supposedly long-dead ex-boyfriend Rick working the pumps. But the baddies are already on to his latest alias and the picture soon explodes, literally, into frenzied action. Mel spends the remainder of the film in a kind of tolerant resignation of these extraordinary, but somehow inevitable circumstances. Goldie, for her part, shrieks a lot, races after Mel and spends most of the picture frightened out of her mind. But through it all a mutual attraction is reawakened. And they have a whole lot of fun.

It appears to have been a happy picture in the making. Gibson said that working with Goldie Hawn was a treat. 'She's spontaneous and funny and added some great ideas in regard to our relationship in the film.' Hawn was much happier working with Gibson than she was with some of the things she was called on to do. That terrifying roller-coaster ride had her protesting so much that the director agreed they would shoot her on only one section of the ride. But to get her to the position she needed to be in meant fork-lifting her up at four o'clock in the morning. 'It was more risky than if I had done the whole ride,' she admitted.

More generally alarming was the scene they shot with wild animals. A massive indoor zoo set, complete with rain forest and three-storey waterfall, was created at Vancouver's Bridge Studios. The difficulty, Badham explained, was that animals do not follow the script: with a non-human cast that included six tigers, a lioness, jaguars, baboons, chimpanzees, four alligators and a 7-foot lizard, one can easily imagine his problems. But this logistical nightmare was more than compensated for by his earlier good fortune when the picture was being cast. He and producer Rob Cohen both made Gibson and Hawn their first choice for the principal roles. But film-makers often have to settle for second or even third choices. 'It's very rare that you read a script, imagine two actors in the lead roles and actually wind up with those two people,' explained Badham. 'But this was one of those occasions where our first choices were the people we got.'

Just as well perhaps since, despite its mauling at the hands of the critics, *Bird on a Wire* turned in a creditable performance, becoming one of the biggest grossing movies of the year, due substantially to the personal drawing power and box-office appeal of Mel Gibson, in particular, and Goldie Hawn.

The quickening pace of Gibson's professional life was again becoming a problem. His alcohol intake was edging up and serious attempts to cut down his heavy smoking had failed. Mel said some time ago that he had tried to quit some fourteen times, but having been a smoker for twenty-five years, it was hard. 'And anyway, I always gain weight,' he complained.

His superstar status meant that he was now committed to helping promote his movies, and he would be shepherded through a string of radio, television and press interviews, which kept him on the move almost round the clock. Contacts with the media can be stressful, even for the biggest stars. Mel Gibson was not alone in finding them mentally sapping, particularly when he would much prefer to be spending time between pictures relaxing on the farm with family and friends. He looked forward to and treasured these intervals. Still in regular touch with his parents, he would have them down to his main Australian home whenever the opportunity arose. He was still close to his brothers and sisters.

New scripts would pile up to be read and the inevitable start date for the next picture would always be looming. Too soon for his own personal well-being, he was back on the treadmill, flying out to Thailand to shoot *Air America*. Gibson was again the all-action man, but with Limato having negotiated a $4.2 million fee, he offered no complaints. The picture is set in 1969 while the Vietnam War is still raging. Over the border in Laos, Air America, boasting some of the world's most skilled civilian pilots, plays a supporting role, airlifting food and supplies to villagers and local anti-communist forces.

The film was based on the book of the same name, written by Christopher Robbins in 1979. In reality Air America was an independent civilian airline owned and operated by the United States Central Intelligence Agency. In the late 1960s the airline's operational headquarters were in Laos, Vietnam's next-door neighbour. From there they ferried supplies to the United States's Far Eastern allies in a bid to stem the advancing tide of communism. Food and medical essentials made up the cargoes. But unofficially drugs and guns were found to be effective currencies that purchased the right level of local anti-communist cooperation; the system depended on generous back-handers for everyone involved, from Air American flyers to top-level government executives, both Laotian and American.

In the film drama, an action-adventure movie with comic elements, Gene Ryack (Gibson), a maverick 'mercenary' veteran of more than one war, flies his missions from a secret air base. He is sticking around long enough to complete a personal gun-running deal that will let him retire in comfort with his Laotian family. Back in the United States, Billy Covington (Robert Downey Jnr), a young, rebellious and highly skilled flyer, has just lost his job and his licence. However, he is offered a unique opportunity in Laos, one that will restore his licence and allow him to fly again.

But in fact he gets much more than he bargained for once Ryack takes him on his orientation flight. He is unprepared for the corruption, endemic in every level of Air America's operations; it even entails drug-dealing collusion between the company's top man and a ruthless local warlord. Eventually Covington decides to blow the drug-running scheme wide open and ropes in a reluctant Ryack, who, while unscrupulous, is basically a decent human being when the chips are down. The consequences of their action are explosive, with their own lives and those of their loved ones in mortal peril. Nancy Travis, who had just finished working with Richard Gere and Andy Garcia in the tense thriller *Internal Affairs*, co-starred as a dedicated refugee camp worker.

Originally Gibson was down to play the younger pilot, which is the more youthful, heroic part. It was Mel who decided that Robert Downey Jnr, nine years younger than Gibson, would better fit the role. *Air America* was directed by the Canadian-born, English-raised Roger Spottiswoode, who took over from Bob Rafelson in the early stages of the project. Spottiswoode's directorial skills were first demonstrated in 1983 with *Under Fire*, a complex and thrilling political drama set against Nicaragua's Sandinista revolution and starring Gene Hackman and Nick Nolte. He found his latest film to be his most complex. 'Working with a national air force (Thailand's) comprising more than 25 aircraft and helicopters, a crew of 500 people forming four different units in remote parts of the world, was certainly more of a challenge than most,' he explained.

It was certainly a challenge for Gibson, a challenge he quickly began to feel he could do without. He had been much more optimistic about the project when it was first presented to him back in comfortable California. The timing was just right for him to do a serious action adventure, and he could identify with his character. But in dense, oppressive and uncomfortable film locations deep in Thailand, he found his positive outlook hard to sustain. He was surprised, nonetheless, to find what a major impact *Mad Max* had made among the locals. They might not have recognized Mel Gibson, but *Mad Max* seemed to be everybody's favourite.

Some of the filming was done in the remote hills of northern Thailand. There was no air-conditioning, no telephone, no hot water, and the nearest hotel was a six-hour drive away. In Chiang Mai, the region's main town, though off the beaten track, a Chinese restaurant became the film's White Rose café. Here the cast faced long and weary hours of shooting, much of it during the hours of darkness. Local customs and conditions added to the pressures. The Thai people were delightful and extremely hospitable, even pushy in their eagerness to please, but Gibson found being openly and frequently accosted by prostitutes, though an accepted part of local life, both irritating and oppressive. Insects and mosquitoes attacked without mercy under cover of darkness, which only added to the discomfort. Gibson was convinced the mosquitoes were armed with machine guns. The unit doctor who travelled out with them had taken no chances and inoculated everyone against just about everything. 'We were pumped with so many holes for inoculations I thought I would leak,' he said.

Learning to fly also made him tense. He had flown a little, but was hardly a cavalier in the air and had no licence. 'I knew a few of the rudimentary things about getting a plane up and what to do with it, but that's all,' he said. Mel somehow kept his natural fears under control and did well enough to lift and land a helicopter without mishap. Against this background his decision to cut out smoking, though well-intentioned, was ill-timed. It just made him bad-tempered. Because he wasn't relaxed he began to drink a few more beers. Heavy and continuous rain threw the schedule off course, and this was followed by a severe earthquake which reached 6.1 on the Richter scale. Cast and crew were tested to the limit.

Mel was desperate to see Robyn, who was on the verge of giving birth again, and fell into a black mood when his request to fly back home to be with her in Australia for a day or two was turned down. Milo's birth was eventually conveyed to him over the telephone by his nine-year-old daughter Hannah, who gave an eye-witness account. Robyn later flew out to see him and, according to reports, brought a complete change of mood. Then, after three long months in Thailand, Gibson was more than happy to be on his way out of the country.

However, he was not quite finished with *Air America*. Six months later, after the picture had been previewed for audiences in America, the producers decided that the ending needed strengthening. By this time Gibson was in London concluding work on *Hamlet*, which would mark a significant development in his career. The *Air America* unit filled in time comfortably enough at the Savoy Hotel. As soon as he finished his outstanding *Hamlet* scenes, they whisked him away to Shepperton studios on the outskirts of London where he joined co-star Robert Downey Jnr for the re-shoot. Mel reportedly received $100,000 for the single day's work, but it is hard to say if the extra work made any difference to the fortunes of *Air America*.

The picture was not a great success, made a comparatively paltry $32 million at the US box office, and the verdict of most critics was lukewarm. Britain's *Film Review* said the most colourful aspect of *Air America* was the exotic Thai locations and went on, '. . . otherwise this wisecracking actioner is a pretty drab affair, with an unsensational storyline, shallow characterisations and little real chemistry between its two stars.' Gibson took his share of the blame, accepting that his was the inferior role; one report alluded to, 'his tendency to look great, but act wooden'. There was certainly smoke in his shared scenes with Downey Jnr, a review suggested, but no sparks.

The film was received with anger and disbelief by writer Christopher Robbins, on whose book, published in 1979, the film had been based. He claimed that the long and detailed research into the Air America airline and its connections with the CIA carried out by Robbins for his book had been largely ignored by the movie-makers. They had trivialized events, where they had covered them at all, and turned an appalling human tragedy of 100,000 deaths into a superficial comedy.

12 . . . to the Classics

Italian film director Franco Zeffirelli, renowned as a man of profound vision and almost limitless ambition, was waiting impatiently for Richard Gere to arrive from Cannes, where he had been attending the annual film festival. It was May 1979, and Zeffirelli wanted to talk to him about his next major project, a major new four-hour stage production of *Hamlet* to be held in Los Angeles later that year. Zeffirelli was already well advanced with his plans. Gere marvelled at the director's ambition and was excited at the prospect of a temporary return to the stage, particularly for such a prestigious production. Once back in New York, he cleared his diary to allow time for preparation and rehearsal.

Zeffirelli was already working with Laurence Olivier on the essential cuts to Shakespeare's original and had Jean Simmons, Amy Irving and E.G. Marshall on standby. Simmons had starred in the film version of *Hamlet* in 1948, which Olivier had produced, directed and starred in, Olivier receiving Oscars for his own performance and Best Picture. But within a few weeks Zeffirelli's plans fell apart when his financial backers pulled out, frightened off by the size of the proposed budget.

Zeffirelli turned his mind to other things, but kept his project on the back-burner. Years later, with the excesses of his earlier vision tempered by failure, and now looking towards Hollywood and a more modest budget, he happened to see Mel Gibson in *Lethal Weapon*. It was the highly dramatic scene in which Gibson puts a gun into his own mouth that stopped Zeffirelli in his tracks. 'Immediately I said: "This is Hamlet. This

143

boy is Hamlet."' Within eighteen months, in January 1989, Zeffirelli, Gibson and agent Ed Limato were sitting down to lunch together at the Four Seasons Hotel in Los Angeles. Limato, who had fixed the meeting, was no stranger to Zeffirelli. More than twenty years before he had been the Italian's third assistant on *The Taming of the Shrew* in Rome. But now the subject was Mel Gibson and whether he would take the title role in the upcoming film version of *Hamlet*.

By this time Zeffirelli felt that the way to attract a younger audience to Shakespeare was to cast a star with whom they could identify. He admitted it was not the easiest part to cast. Sean Connery could have done it, but he was really outside the age range. He looked at Robert de Niro as a possibility, but found he was booked up for two years on other projects. 'I began to look at youngish actors, and I landed on this extraordinary Gibson,' he said. He carefully sat through *Mad Max*, *Gallipoli* and *Lethal Weapon* two or three times and felt that Gibson had the potential to take on Shakespeare. He liked the energy, violence and danger of his part in *Mad Max*, seeing something Elizabethan in his character. That, plus his sensitivity in *Gallipoli* and what Zeffirelli recognized as his potential as a great tragedian in *Lethal Weapon*, helped his candidature as the director turned over the idea in his mind.

For his part, Mel was inspired by the possibility of doing *Hamlet* and perhaps a little flattered that he should be under serious consideration by someone of Zeffirelli's status. For the Italian director had been involved with Shakespeare, on and off, during most of his film and theatre career. At the same time Gibson had certain misgivings. He quietly expressed some doubts about its chances as a movie. 'You know, Shakespeare and film don't necessarily mix,' he said. And he knew only too well how demanding Shakespeare can be for an actor. 'I like the story, but it's incredibly difficult; and I wanted to know that I could do it,' he said. More to the point, perhaps, was his state of physical and mental exhaustion. He had, after all, just done three pictures in a row. Now to confront a role where his performance would be up for comparison with some of the best classic actors of all time, including Olivier, seemed an awesome burden.

But Gibson was not just the superficial celluloid hero known by most of his massive cinema following. Unlike some of his Hollywood contemporaries he had served that long apprenticeship in the classics while at the National Institute of Dramatic Art in Sydney, the Nimrod Theatre and elsewhere. It would be a major challenge, certainly. He would be leaving himself open to all kinds of contempt and ridicule from snooty critics.

On the other hand, he had enough artistic savvy to know that, professionally, it was a challenge he really ought to take. As Gibson said at the time: 'It was a question of whether I'd pick up the challenge or let it go by; to be or not to be . . . Hamlet, if I can put it that way.' But really, Mel's mind was already made up. To his agent's surprise and alarm, 'we shook hands on it right there and then,' during lunch at the Four Seasons Hotel. It was a unique occasion, because never before had Gibson committed himself to a film offer after just one meeting. 'It's amazing just what a dish of spaghetti can do,' he joked.

Zeffirelli saw his new *Hamlet* as a means of restoring a personal reputation that had lately suffered in the wake of his last two studio productions, *The Champ* (1979) and *Endless Love* (1981). Neither was much appreciated by the critics. Moreover, the flamboyance and eccentricities that contributed to his great reputation also tended to inhibit potential financial backers.

Now aged sixty-eight, Zeffirelli knew that a major triumph was imperative for him to retain his standing in Hollywood. With Shakespeare, with *Hamlet*, he felt himself to be on secure ground. He had first directed *Hamlet* some twenty-five years earlier for a stage production in the United States. In 1967 he delighted cinema audiences by bringing together Elizabeth Taylor and Richard Burton in a lusty, vibrant version of *The Taming of the Shrew*. A year later, also on screen, he swept tradition aside by ignoring experienced Shakespearean actors and casting Leonard Whiting and England's Argentinian-born Olivia Hussey, then only seventeen years old, in his acclaimed version of *Romeo and Juliet*. The picture lost some of the poetry and power of Shakespeare's original language, but brought the adolescent passion to the fore, in beautifully photographed Italian locations.

Zeffirelli loved to flout tradition. His *Hamlet* would be driven by his own interpretation. But even he realized from the start that his yen for overblown, overlong sagas would need to

145

be disciplined. Four hours was far too long so he and co-screen-writer Christopher de Vore worked closely with the Royal Shakespeare Company's John Barton, aiming ambitiously for two hours maximum, but wrestled long and in the end unsuc-cessfully to improve on 2 hrs 30 mins.

This classic tale of murder and revenge has been told many times on stage, screen and television but, as Gibson pointed out: 'We felt we had our own *Hamlet* to tell. I thought the 20th cen-tury medium of film would make a really interesting contrast with the 400-year-old-text.' It was to be a *Hamlet* for the 1990s, explained Gibson and Zeffirelli, as the director began lining up his strong, mostly British cast: Alan Bates (recruited to play King Claudius), Paul Scofield (the Ghost), Ian Holm (Polonius) and Helena Bonham-Carter (Ophelia). From America, to play Hamlet's mother, Queen Gertrude, came Glenn Close, a sur-prising choice after her lustful role in *Dangerous Liaisons*. Surprising, too, because, despite playing Hamlet's mother she is in fact only nine years older than Mel.

However, even with such a formidable cast and such big names as Gibson and Close committed to the project, raising the relatively modest $15.5 million budget for the seventy-day shoot was tough. Gibson and Close were both said to be working at much below their normal market rate (Mel would eventually receive $700,000), and producer Dyson Lovell later explained that no studio with thoughts of commercial gain would touch it. Mel had built up a good deal of confidence as a bankable star, but potential financiers still clung to their doubts about linking a modern action hero with Shakespeare. Nor, at this point, was a Zeffirelli project seen as a fashionable investment. His most recent movie, *Young Toscanini*, in 1988, never found a distribu-tor and his film operas, *La Traviata* (1982) and *Otello* (1986), though meritorious in themselves, were seen as too minority-interest.

In the end Mel's own company, Icon Productions, which he had formed with his accountant Bruce Davey, after the break-up of his earlier association with Pat Lovell, delivered a good pro-portion of the finance. Warner Brothers, with a sharp eye to securing the future career of their megastar hero, also found some of the funding. After all, there was always a danger he could defect to another studio.

Shooting began, appropriately enough, on the 426th anniversary of Shakespeare's birth, 23 April 1990, at Dover Castle, built by the Normans in the twelfth century. This great castle was not regarded by the film-makers as being totally representative of Shakespeare's fabled Elsinore, on the north coast of Zealand, Denmark's easternmost island. Their search had taken them all over Europe, but in the end the historic ruins at Dover were selected, along with those of Blackness Castle in West Lothian, and Dunnottar Castle, perched on an isolated rock near Stonehaven, just south of Aberdeen. All three were photographed so as to form one composite building. Tons of coal dust mixed with water were transported on to each site and poured over the buildings in order to give them a uniformly dark and weathered exterior. Studio work was carried out at Shepperton, conveniently close to London.

Zeffirelli had firm views about bringing his *Hamlet* to life, and he assembled some top craftsmen – cinematographer David Watkin, designer Dante Ferretti and composer Ennio Morricone: Oscar winners all. Said Zeffirelli:

> My aim was to make the story clear without mutilating the original. We wanted to make *Hamlet* easier to understand because he has so often been misunderstood on stage. *Hamlet* in the Elizabethan theatre was violence, excitement, fun, sport and singing – those characters were full of vitality. Before you take the man away from life, you must show his life force. Then the audience will be doubly shocked by the tragedy.

After the film had finished shooting Zeffirelli was satisfied he had achieved his objective. 'I think that Mel brings out those dual qualities in Hamlet – the vitality and humour before the storm he faces after his father's murder. He also had an ironic sense of humour that perfectly matches Hamlet's. We can never forget that the play is often very trenchant and funny.'

Mel knew from the start that he had committed himself to probably the most arduous, demanding and difficult role of his career. In the beginning he found it difficult deciding how, precisely, he should play the character in the context of Zeffirelli's production. He was tired and jaded after months of continuous film-making. Adding to the strain was his desire to moderate his

147

smoking and drinking. Once again, a major influence in keeping his feet on the ground and events in perspective was having Robyn and the family with him in England. He settled them into a sumptuous eighteen bedroom house in an acre of land in the Home Counties, close to the studios. Before shooting began he and Robyn took themselves off to the calm of Henlow Grange, just north of London in Bedfordshire, for a few days of relaxation and health promotion under expert guidance.

Gibson viewed Hamlet as a pivotal role in his career. It demanded physical strength and powerful lungs for those intense, often tongue-twisting Shakespearean passages. Fully committed to the role he cut out cigarettes and worked assiduously with a specialist voice coach, discovering just how hard it was to leave behind all traces of those Aussie, and more recently acquired American vowel sounds. He worked on his voice to build up the degree of diction necessary for a classical role. He quickly discovered that playing Hamlet, despite the changes made by Zeffirelli, called for intense mental concentration and a strong physical capacity. He had to work hard on his fencing technique, master the art of sword fighting and horse riding. Surely the latter was not a problem for someone who, in spirit at least, was almost as much a cattle farmer as an actor? But the truth was, Mel could not really ride very well at all. 'I normally use an off-road motor bike on the farms,' he explained.

The director was bold in his approach, but disciplined by the dictates of a restricted budget. Rather than tinker here and adjust there, he would take out whole scenes. 'What I'm trying to do with *Hamlet*,' explained Zeffirelli, 'is to unleash the energy it contains and let it explode. I want to show that power to the audience.' He admitted that he saw *Hamlet* as his ticket back to dramatic cinema.

At the early rehearsals, when the actors met to read through the script for the first time, there was some feeling of unease and a little tension. The cast fell instinctively into two groups, with the theatre types like Bates, Holm and Scofield sensing a mutual kinship; Gibson and Close, on the other hand, were very much the Hollywood input, although Close, like Gibson, had performed Shakespeare early in her career. Curiously enough, as the reading started Gibson and Close found themselves taking up positions on one side of the table while Bates, Holm and

Scofield made for the chairs opposite. However, this implicit distance rapidly disintegrated as everyone got on with the business of making the picture.

According to the acutely aware Zeffirelli, it was only the method of working which distinguished their backgrounds. 'When you talk with the English actors you know what they are going to give you,' he explained. 'They will tell you in advance about any surprises they might have for you, anything which might be unpredictable. But anything unpredictable from Gibson and Close came at you out of the blue.'

Mel soon settled into the script and gained enormous respect from just about everyone on the set. Ian Holm voiced what many felt about Gibson when he said that he had nothing but admiration for him. 'It's a hell of a thing for a megastar of his magnitude to put himself on the line by playing Hamlet with a lot of Brits . . . and he is doing fine.' In a sense it was rather like having, say, Kenneth Branagh playing Buffalo Bill, but Gibson was soon performing Hamlet with as much concentration and intensity as he dredges up for all his roles. Zeffirelli put his finger on it. 'He is always looking, searching. Sometimes you see him in a corner of the studio going around like a madman. It's wonderful, really wonderful.'

Though thoroughly professional on the set, and despite his classical costume, cropped dyed hair, neatly grown moustache and beard, Gibson maintained his reputation for fooling around and breaking the tension with some idiot action or off-the-cuff comment. One incident concerned a long shot in which Gibson was supposed to stare at Bonham-Carter as he staggers, crazed and grief-stricken, from the room. The trouble was, because his eyes were locked on hers, he couldn't really see where he was going. Twice he walked smack into a large, wooden cupboard. Almost straight away Mel went into a couple of pratfalls and started cracking haemorrhoid jokes with the crew. Soon he had the scene right. Bonham-Carter said: 'He's a real clown, a buffoon. He is so relaxed when you are with him.' Close resorted to kissing him, impassively and mechanically as 'the most effective way to stop him telling those terrible jokes'.

As always Mel resorted to humour as much to break his own tension as to help others, burdened as he was by intense pressure and responsibility. The role extended him physically as well as mentally. His costume, which he was sewn into, made him sweat greatly under the studio lights and he lost as much as ten pounds bodyweight in a day. He was irritated and in considerable pain when a chronic back problem suddenly flared up when he was lifting someone; filming had to be delayed for twenty-four hours.

Oases of contentment and delight came in the form of the occasional visits to the set by Robyn and the family. Their presence never failed to restore him in mind and body. He also had his parents, Hutton and Anne, fly over from Australia to spend several weeks with them at their rented home. But for all that, the physical and mental strain was slowly taking its toll. He was generous in his praise of his co-stars, though in some ways he remained in awe of the wealth of classical acting talent surrounding him – actors who had become steeped in Shakespeare through much of their working lives. He found their admiration of his work gratifying, but it did little to ease the burden.

The odd joky response would reveal something of the inner Gibson. Asked if he had received any tips from the veterans around him, Mel gave a dazed nod. 'Even the cameraman one time picked me up on pronunciation,' he said. Zeffirelli had warned him of the mountainous task ahead. 'I promised him from the beginning that it would be worse and worse and worse for him . . . the problem is that once you open the discussion on *Hamlet* you will never be satisfied. The more you conquer, the more you feel you miss.' The spirit of *Hamlet* was always there, close at hand, no matter how many takes were needed, how dispirited or tired you felt.

An enormous sense of relief came when filming ended. He took Robyn off to Paris for a couple of days' shopping and relaxation, before embarking on an exhausting worldwide promotion tour in support of the picture. Gibson playing Hamlet had sparked off a phenomenal sense of expectancy, and Mel did his bit dutifully, politely answering journalists' questions and keeping that essential twinkle in his eye. They wanted to talk to him about his private life, about events long since past, but always he managed to bring the topic back to *Hamlet*. He remained composed and kept in mind what he had said earlier, that he did not think the purists would be offended, although some licence had been taken. 'That's inevitable when you're taking a great play to the screen,' he pointed out. 'But remember, there's no absolute right way to do it, considering too that we have to open it out for film.'

Particularly fascinating was his hour-long educational video called *Mel Gibson Goes back to School*, in which Mel chats easily and casually to tenth-grade students of University High in Los Angeles. Showing no signs of strain, and full of enthusiasm for *Hamlet*, it showed Gibson at his best.

Working closely with his young audience, he asked them to abandon their preconceived antipathy towards the film's Shakespearean language, encouraging them to look beyond the surface at the beauty of colour, syntax and rhythm in the play. He discussed *Hamlet* in language they understood. It's a great story, he told them, '. . . eight violent deaths, murder, incest, adultery, a mad woman, poison, revenge, and swordfights'. It was a telling demonstration of his natural ability to get on with people. His own enthusiasm was infectious and his young audience responded readily. He had them thinking seriously about Shakespeare and *Hamlet*, perhaps for the very first time in their lives. 'There are so many layers to *Hamlet*,' he explained, 'so many of those classic sayings still in use today . . . to thine own self be true, for example.'

In helping the scholars to understand *Hamlet*, to make sense of it all, he demonstrated with great conviction his own off-the-cuff knowledge of the subject. He projected friendliness and dynamism, together with a fine understanding of young people. He not only explained what he could about Shakespeare, but suggested questions for debate. Some of the questions he could not answer because, as he explained, Shakespeare doesn't always provide easy solutions. But asking the question and talking about it was the important issue.

Almost everyone closely involved with *Hamlet* – Gibson, Zeffirelli, Close, Bonham-Carter, Holm, Bates, Scofield, the studio crew and so on – considered that the film had been well and seriously made; it was lively, interesting, dramatic, entertaining. But soon the reviewers would have their say.

In North America the response was much more upbeat than many had dared to hope, with influential papers like the *New York Times, New York Post, Toronto Globe and Mail* and *USA Today* posting excellent notices. Gibson must have allowed himself a wry smile on reading the *New York News*, however: 'Those who come to mock this strutting Hollywood player may be surprised by his vigorous self-assured performance.' The *New York Post* and *USA Today* weighed in with, respectively: 'Yes, Mel Gibson makes a very good Hamlet. By my troth, a very good Hamlet . . .', and, 'It's a triumph few could have predicted.' Best of all appeared in the *New York Times*:

> Mel Gibson's Hamlet is strong, intelligent and safely beyond ridicule. He is a visceral Hamlet, tortured by his own thoughts and passions, confused by his recognition of evil, a Hamlet whose emotions are raw yet who retains the desperate wit to act mad. He is by far the best part of Mr Zeffirelli's sometimes slick but always lucid and beautifully cinematic version of the play.

Mel travelled back to Australia with his confidence boosted, his energies and spirits restored. It is often at such times that the duality of his personality is most pronounced, being witty, bold, basic, occupying the high ground one minute, then retiring, modest, deep-thinking, embarrassed and ordinary the next. NIDA scholarship students asked him about the cynical way in which the tabloids had responded to the news that he would play Hamlet. His response delighted them. 'Who cares?' he rasped. 'I don't. I'm rich.' And when trying to explain to a reporter why *Hamlet* was important to him, he said that he loved Shakespeare and the world needs more Shakespeare – 'because it is full of wisdom, wit and beauty. We need more of that and less of the other . . . like a weekend trip to a knocking shop.'

Yet it was a far less brash Mel Gibson who arrived modestly for the Australian premiere of the movie in Sydney and, ignoring the seats reserved for VIPs, settled himself quietly in a position on the side. When the lights went up to resounding applause at the end of the screening, Mel had already made his discreet exit. In America he won the Shakespeare Theatre's *Will Award* in Washington for *Hamlet*, presented in part because his performance helped introduce film audiences and children to classical theatre. 'It's rare that a person with that amount of celebrity will lay themselves on the line,' said the theatre's artistic director, Michael Kahn. Previous winners of the *Will Award*,

Playing the tortured Hamlet
in Franco Zeffirelli's 1991
version of the classic tale.
The modern hero's convincing performance surprised
many people who knew
little of his classical training

As action man Martin
Riggs in *Lethal Weapon 3*
(1992). Mel Gibson gained
enormous worldwide com-
mercial success from the
Lethal Weapon pictures.
The spectacular stunt
sequences were an impor-
tant feature of the movies

Action and romance with Rene Russo in *Lethal Weapon 3* (1992)

With Jamie Lee Curtis in the romantic thriller *Forever Young* (1992) in which he plays a test pilot frozen from 1939 to 1992

Gibson directing a film for the first time in *The Man Without a Face* (1993). He also starred in the film

In the classic quick-fire Western comedy *Maverick* (1994) Gibson, as the charming con man gambler, stars with Jodie Foster and James Garner in a hilarious presentation

The beautiful French actress Sophie Marceau in *Braveheart* (1995)

A tense scene from the 1997 suspense-thriller *Conspiracy Theory* in which Mel co-stars for the first time with Julia Roberts

In the riveting, tension-packed *Ransom* (1997) Gibson is a business tycoon who takes matters into his own hands when his son is kidnapped. The picture was an enormous box office triumph

which was established in 1988, include the late director, Joseph Papp, and actors Kevin Kline, Christopher Plummer and Kenneth Branagh.

On a broader front, *Hamlet* had convincingly overturned the somewhat flippant notion first expressed some years before, that Mel Gibson was simply too good-looking to be a good actor.

In Britain, where Shakespeare is woven deeply into the fabric of the nation, the film was given closer, more critical scrutiny. The English critics had hardly been inspired at the prospect of an Australian/Hollywood icon passing himself off as a messenger of The Bard, but their reaction, if predictably lukewarm, was less hostile than might have been feared. Gibson pleased his fans by attending the British premiere of *Hamlet*, held on 19 April 1991 at the Odeon in London's West End.

Whenever Gibson felt the need to recharge those physical and emotional batteries he turned his back on the California that had now, inevitably, become established as home. For home is where the work is. *Hamlet* had been a fulfilling, though draining experience, but now it was done. He did not regret his decision to confront the challenge. In a sense he felt a better person for doing just that. But rest and relaxation were long overdue. It was high time to retreat, to spend those long, leisurely days with Robyn and the family on their Australian farm at Tangambalanga, near the willow-shaded banks of the Kiewa River in Victoria. But this time, he knew, it would be different. This time he knew that his mother would not be there.

13 Hollywood's Brightest Star

Anne Gibson died in December 1990. She was diagnosed diabetic with a heart condition and had been unwell for some time, but her death at sixty-nine was unexpected. Mel was devastated. He had just finished post-production work on *Hamlet* and was in Los Angeles promoting the film when the news came through. He took the first available flight to Australia, touching down after twenty-four hours, weary and saddened.

His mind spanned the years: his childhood and the move from America to Australia; the strong personal example handed down by his father and mother; the happy home life with its strong basis in religion; his first unsteady steps with those early movies; the unstinting love of his parents for all their children through the ups and downs of their lives; and his own personal love for them.

Though not given to flamboyant displays of emotion, his mother had been warmed and excited by his rise to international celebrity status. He knew that. But how proud she would have been to see him climb even higher as a widely acclaimed Hamlet. Fancy, our Mel playing Shakespeare in the movies! But it was not to be. She never saw the picture. Adding to Mel's sorrow was that just a short time before her death, he had moved his mother and father into a property on his extended Tangambalanga estate so that they could be together more often. Hutton would stay on after his wife's death to look after the place when Mel and his family were away.

Mel was deeply affected by his mother's death. Some would

claim that it had a particular poignancy for him because it occurred so soon after playing Hamlet, in which the emotional intensity of the mother-son relationship is a key theme. Back on the farm he gathered round him people who were a great source of comfort and understanding. To neighbours and friends living close by, he was never the big unapproachable star. He never traded his fame. He was a ranch owner just like most of them. They talked about cattle and the kids. And as before, when the press and others tried to break into his private world, his friends again became a barrier, turning away any unwelcome visitors long before they could approach Mel.

But after the funeral, and left with his own private grief, Mel showed that megastars are no different from anyone else. He felt the vacuum, mourned her passing, but, like other mortals, found that life has to go on. He completed his schedule of promotion for *Hamlet* and then went back to his farm to spend some time relaxing and pondering the future. *Mad Max* and *Lethal Weapon* had transformed him into a major international box-office star. He had proved how successful he could be with romance and comedy. *Hamlet* had added a deeper, more serious dimension. The nineties beckoned with a host of opportunities. It was director Roger Spottiswoode who said after *Hamlet*: 'Mel's asking price will be ten or eleven million dollars.' Others pointed out what almost everyone knew: that he never needed to work again.

But despite his enormous wealth, the nineties signalled an ever quickening pace in Mel Gibson's professional life. For it was in February 1991 that Warner Brothers signed their remarkable $42 million deal with Mel for a four-picture partnership. Mel would also receive royalties, and his company, Icon Productions, would produce the films. He would also have the opportunity to direct.

First, though, he returned as action-man supreme in *Lethal Weapon 3*. For his pains Gibson received a $10 million fee, almost three times his combined payment for the two earlier *Weapon* pictures. Richard Donner was once more directing, he and Joel Silver were the producers and the screenplay was by Jeffrey Boam and Robert Mark Kamen. The picture brought Mel (Martin Riggs) and Danny Glover (Roger Murtaugh) together once more and picked up on their developing relationship. This time Riggs is an honorary member of the Murtaugh household, now that he has exorcised the ghosts of his past and finally laid the tragedy of his wife's death to rest. But as ever, Gibson is the mad-dog detective while Glover is his long-suffering sidekick.

The picture provided plenty of humour and lots of action. It resisted the obvious temptation to rely too heavily on technical gimmickry for its own sake, but did create a sense of spectacle and visual impact through some wonderful and extraordinary special effects, including imploding buildings, high-speed free-way chases against traffic, 80-foot falls and the torching of a dozen houses on an abandoned estate. The action was fast and the incidents were frequent. The clever blend of wisecracking and action was underpinned by a plot with several unexpected twists and turns. A series of real and emotional explosions take the pair from plain clothes to beat-pounding and then towards the very edge of survival. As before, the mature Murtaugh is circumspect and cautious, while Riggs is the younger, more reckless chancer.

The plot is not all that important. After a long and distinguished career with the Los Angeles Police Department, Murtaugh is just seven days away from retirement and looking forward to it. While most officers would relax during this run-up to peaceful civilian life, Murtaugh is offered no such luxury. For he and Riggs, unorthodox as ever, are currently investigating the disappearance of a cache of illegal firearms that should have been destroyed. Stolen from police lock-ups, these weapons have begun to resurface on the streets, most recently in the hands of street-gang youths. At the centre of events is a corrupt ex-cop played by British actor Stuart Wilson.

Joe Pesci was once again recruited to the cast, along with a new love interest in the shapely form of Rene Russo, who plays Lorna Cole from the Internal Affairs Department. A reckless, fast-talking, karate-kicking cop with nerves of steel, she is just the type to infuriate Martin Riggs. But she proves she packs the know-how to stimulate Riggs' interest in the opposite sex again, and eventually they fall in love with each other.

There are problems in doing the third movie in a sequence. 'The challenge,' said director Donner, 'is to keep the characters honest, to keep the humour in the piece and to keep you caring about the people in it.' Mel also had his say:

There's an interesting reversal of roles in this one, because something happens to Murtaugh and Riggs is called upon to pull him out of a deep emotional tailspin, much the way Roger had to help Martin in the original *Lethal Weapon*. We've seen these guys go through a lot, from one end of the emotional scale to the other. In a way, it's an exploration of what all friends do for each other, but on a grand scale.

In some ways it was the least violent and gutsy of the trilogy. Just sixteen people were killed this time round, against twenty-nine in *LW2*, only five cars were wrecked (fourteen in *LW2*) and there were just four explosions (against seven in the earlier film), though the final effort is so massive it could count as four or five on its own. Nobody was surprised to see *Lethal Weapon* back on the screens and its welcome was assured. However, one reviewer thought it was showing definite signs of wear, while another suggested it was significantly lacking its predecessors' subtlety, finesse and sense of purpose.

But the paying customers seemed to have few complaints. They probably expected a bit of 'tongue in cheek' and a good deal of action and adventure. Certainly, the film did not take itself too seriously, despite costing a formidable $40 million to make. A good investment? Absolutely, because the response was exceptional even by the most optimistic forecasts. It took $33 million in the first three days of its release in the United States (most pictures don't make that much ever); and within two weeks the US take was more than $70 million. It recorded the second biggest opening success in history, topping *Terminator 2* on its first weekend. *Lethal Weapon 3* would go on to make more than $160 million at the US box office alone and exceed $700 million (some £500 million) worldwide.

Mel Gibson had confirmed his status as one of the biggest names in Hollywood and the most bankable movie star in the world. His contract with Warner Brothers had also helped him to become one of the most powerful people in Hollywood, with the authority to set his own agenda. At the time the contract was signed a Warners spokesman, questioned about the huge amount of money being offered, stated that money was not the problem, but securing Mel Gibson for the studio was.

Film ideas and scripts were now pouring in for his considera-tion, and his company, Icon Productions, was inundated.

Material was being written with him specifically in mind. And he had his own ideas too. Some kind of western, perhaps. Certainly, he was on the look-out for a project which would provide a sharp contrast to his previous all-action work. He talked it over with his long-time friend and business partner at Icon, Bruce Davey, and the development side of the company was put on red alert to come up with a project that would appeal to Gibson.

Screenwriter Jeffrey Abrams had produced a somewhat bizarre story combining a touch of science fiction with romance and adventure. Gibson was first intrigued, then strongly committed to the story. Warner Brothers, keen to retain Gibson's good will, bought the script from Abrams as a specific project for Mel. It was a historic deal: the fee, an astonishing $2 million, was at that time the largest sum ever paid for a screenplay of that kind. The film, originally titled *The Rest of Daniel*, but changed to *Forever Young*, took Mel back into the air as dare-devil test pilot, Daniel McCormick.

It is 1939 and Daniel McCormick is his own man, taking the world by the tail and having the time of his life flying B-25s for the newly formed Air Corps. His loyal buddy is Harry Finley (George Wendt), and his childhood sweetheart and beautiful soulmate, Helen, is played by Isabel Glasser. But the outgoing extrovert has one problem: he becomes tongue-tied when it comes to popping the 'will you marry me?' question.

So events overtake them. Tragedy strikes and snatches Helen away. Unwilling to go on alone, he volunteers for a top-secret scientific experiment conducted by his friend, Harry, which leaves him cryogenically frozen for fifty years. When the perfectly preserved airman reawakens, the world has changed so much it is hardly recognizable . . . though he does recognize his attraction to single mother Claire (Jamie Lee Curtis) who, along with her son Nat (Elijah Wood), becomes an important aspect of his life.

The film was sometimes trailed as a time-travel movie. Gibson did not see it like that. 'This is really a love story,' he explained. 'The fun of this heroic guy thrown into an unfamiliar world fascinated me. But I wanted to stay away from doing a time travel movie.' It is debatable whether, without Gibson, *Forever Young* would have succeeded in attracting the punters in sufficient numbers. As it turned out it secured a US box office gross of around $50 million. Said *Empire* magazine: 'It is a film of performances rather than ingenious ideas or inventive action. And it is yet another smart change of pace for Gibson, who proves again that he can carry off almost anything with apparent conviction but with a definite "Isn't this a wheeze?" twinkle in those baby blue eyes.'

Throughout his movie career Mel had succumbed to spells of frantic action and heavy commitment, but during the early to mid 1990s his workload was more sustained, better planned. But still nerve-janglingly hectic. *Lethal Weapon 3* and *Forever Young* were released in 1992, to be followed by *The Man Without a Face* in 1993 and *Maverick* in 1994.

Often unpredictable in his choice of material, Gibson has responded to almost every kind of acting challenge, from urban thrillers like *Lethal Weapon* to Shakespeare's *Hamlet*, from period dramas such as *Gallipoli* and *The Bounty* to the sci-fi action of *Mad Max*, and from sensitive character pieces like *Tim* and *The River*, to knockabout comedy (*Bird on a Wire*) and contemporary thrillers (*Tequila Sunrise* and *Mrs Soffel*).

In 1993, and still not forty years old, he fulfilled his long-held ambition of becoming a film director. *The Man Without a Face*, a social drama about an ex-convict indicted for child abuse trying to start life afresh in a small town, was a difficult choice. Responsible for bringing to life the sensitive subject of life-affirming friendships between two loners in small-town America, he found himself in conflict with one of acting's unwritten laws: never work with children or animals.

This touching tale from the sixties was an adaptation of a well-read novel by Isabelle Holland. Chuck, played by twelve-year-old Nick Stahl, is a confused, fatherless boy who lives with his much married and flirtatious mother and two resentful half-sisters. He is desperate to escape to a prep school where his now deceased father once held sway, but there seems little hope since he has already failed the entrance examination. The boy secretly enlists the aid of a disfigured recluse, Justin McLeod (*The Man Without a Face*), as his tutor, but the move inadvertently brings the fury of his hometown upon his new-found friend.

Understanding and mutual trust are emotions the two characters have never experienced before, but find in their relationship with each other. Gibson showed something of his directorial precision early on by purposely changing the twelve-year old Stahl into a thirteen-year-old for his film character. He reckoned that first teenage year to be more indicative of the start of growing and worrying, the emotional changes, the highs and lows.

Much of the ten-week shoot took place in and around small and remote communities in Maine, but as usual Mel had Robyn and his children travel across America to be with him. Gibson had chosen a tough assignment on which to cut his director's teeth, for he was acting as well and the lead role was a demanding one. Each day began with a three-hour make-up session that transformed the handsome Gibson into the tragically scarred, burns victim McLeod. Said Gibson at the time: 'It was like a three-ring circus. Getting up at five o'clock every morning to put the prosthetics on, going out and winding up the shots and then actually being in it, wasn't easy. But I'm not complaining. I like hard work.'

However, Gibson had been looking to lighten his load once he moved into the director's chair. Rumour had it that he twice tried to coax well-known actors into taking on the role of McLeod, eventually and somewhat grudgingly taking over himself as a last resort. But he found the experience more difficult than he had imagined. 'You have to wear too many hats and it just drives you crazy,' he explained, adding after filming was completed that if he ever directed another film he would not act in it.

The original book of *The Man Without a Face* had been optioned several times before Canadian writer Malcolm MacRury set to work on changing it into a screenplay. Gibson had been given MacRury's script to look at as far back as 1990 when, even then, he was searching for a strong character-driven piece with which to make his directorial debut.

Once a deal was struck Icon Productions spent more than two years developing the movie, and in particular, lightening it, especially the ending. The film proved a shrewd choice and was well respected on its release in the United States in August 1993, though it was never expected to generate the colossal audiences of Gibson's action-man movies. *The Man Without a Face* also took Gibson, with Robyn and the family, to France for a few months, where he gained his first experience of vital post-production work.

The days when Mel Gibson had to forage around looking for suitable movie material were long since gone. A whole organization, through Icon Productions in particular, was now established to search for and look at scripts and ideas that might be put forward as possible Gibson projects. Mel still hankered after a western. The enormous success in 1990 of Kevin Costner's *Dances with Wolves* and of Clint Eastwood's *Unforgiven* constituted a minor renaissance of the genre and helped to fuel Gibson's ambition. He knew that a well chosen western would work for him too, but what he eventually decided to do was a big surprise for his associates as well as something of a disappointment, certainly at first.

Maverick, even at the height of its popular success, had never been much more than an average, run-of-the-mill television potboiler. Picking it up after all those years was seen as a tepid, ill-thought-out response to Mel's desire to play a western on the big screen. But according to Bruce Davey it was Mel himself who came up with the idea. 'Mel dropped hints once in a while about a western he was developing,' explained Davey. 'Then one day he simply came to me with *Maverick*.' But the roots of the decision on *Maverick* were embedded in the days when Gibson was filming *Hamlet* and Davey investigated the rights to the Warner Brothers television series. 'Maverick is an easy-going guy, a pretty cool customer. I thought that sort of suits Mel,' explained Davey. Gibson remembers watching the re-runs as a child in Australia. 'I was fascinated by westerns and *Maverick* was my favourite.'

It was an astute move on Gibson's part to hire William Goldman to script the *Maverick* project. Goldman was already a Hollywood icon after penning such screen classics as *A Bridge Too Far*, *Marathon Man* and *Indecent Proposal*. He received Academy Awards for *Butch Cassidy and the Sundance Kid* in 1969 and *All the President's Men* in 1976. Gathering an expert and influential team around him, Gibson brought in director/producer Richard Donner, who had handled all three *Lethal Weapons*, Jodie Foster, the winner of two Academy Awards for *Silence of the Lambs*, and – a neat piece of casting – James Garner, television's original Maverick, who had also featured in the highly successful *The Rockford Files*. Garner was Gibson's choice and he stepped in after Paul Newman had

161

turned down the role. Foster was a surprise choice, giving a firm yes just three weeks before shooting was due to start. Meg Ryan was originally down for the role, but she cried off, wanting to spend more time with actor husband, Dennis Quaid, and their child. Foster, already an accomplished director and actress, said it was the unpredictability of her role as the beguiling Annabelle Bransford that she found intriguing. 'It was so unlike anything I had ever done and that's probably the reason I was attracted to it,' she explained. 'I was really interested in doing a comedy that was light-hearted and witty.' It was now eighteen years since Foster had done comedy, as a thirteen-year-old in *Bugsy Malone*. Old-stager James Coburn was drafted in to play The Commodore.

Principal photography for *Maverick* began in El Mirage, California, on a dry lake bed in blistering heat. The scene has Maverick dangling precariously from a solitary tree in a hang-man's noose, with a clump of snakes, both real and animatron-ic, close at hand. Gibson and Donner found it nostalgic, for the location marked the beginning of their highly successful part-nership, when shooting the original *Lethal Weapon*. Other loca-tion shots included historic Lone Pine and the Alabama Hills, in California, the famous backdrop for countless early westerns, from Fatty Arbuckle's *The Roundup* in 1920. The Lone Ranger, Roy Rogers, Tom Mix had all been shot there. They were ideal locations, according to Mel, 'beautiful scenery, fresh air and I could go home to the family every weekend!' The banks of the Crystal River and Lake Powell in Oklahoma were among the other locations.

The Navajo Indian Reservation in Arizona was used for the famous runaway stagecoach sequence, which would go on to acquire almost cult status among *aficionados*, while less than 90 miles (54 km) from the north rim of the Grand Canyon, Gibson dangled from a small ledge high above the Colorado River. Said Richard Donner: 'With Mel, if you set a shot and have to walk away, when you come back he's done what the stuntmen are doing.' Filming ended with more location work in the Yosemite Valley and on the Warner Brothers sound stages in Burbank.

The plot is full of fun and improbable adventure which seems to tail off towards the end – until the finale with its unexpected pay-off. Gibson plays the eponymous hero Bret Maverick, a charming gambler with an astonishing capacity for getting into trouble. The scene shifts from the smoky recesses of a saloon poker table to the untamed canyons and prairies of the Wild West, fabulous riverboats and, eventually, to the embrace of the beautiful, wily con woman Annabelle Bransford (Foster). All along the way, Maverick encounters almost every western peril imaginable, from bar room brawls and a runaway stagecoach to American Indians and rattlesnakes, not to mention the unflappable lawman, Marshall Zane Cooper (James Garner), who seems to have the particular knack of anticipating Maverick's every move.

As Maverick decides to pit his talent – and his bankroll – against the best in the west in a lucrative poker championship, the paths of Maverick, Annabelle and 'Coop' become more closely intertwined. Gibson glides through the film with a beautifully disarming smile and the biggest tongue-in-cheek imaginable. Perhaps the funniest sequence is when the 'injuns' arrive on the scene, a moment of exquisite timing. Highly amusing in a quiet way is Annabelle's persistent habit of getting Maverick's name slightly wrong, calmly calling him Bert all the time, instead of Bret. His corrections and injured expression are all to no avail.

According to Mel, it was an entertaining film to make. 'It's a send-up,' he said. Once on the set he found he had a gun-twirling partner in James Garner. 'Working with Jim is a lot of fun,' said Gibson during a break in filming. 'We've just been horsing around ever since we started. The two could often be seen sharing tricks and spinning guns in and out of their holsters.

A fan of sleight-of-hand tricks, Gibson found manipulating cards to be more difficult than twirling six-shooters. 'It's hard to work a deck of cards,' he said. 'Guns are easier. They're more like juggling.' The game of poker, however, did not seem to create the same difficulties for Gibson – or the rest of the cast, for that matter. On any given day games of five-card draw and seven-card stud were in full swing during lighting setups. Both Gibson and Jodie Foster became proficient at the patented James Garner one-handed shuffle. Gibson explained how it's done: 'Holding the deck in one hand, you squeeze the cards out of the middle of the deck with your thumb and little finger and then

163

place them on the top of the deck.'

Donner explained that *Maverick* was made to be seen by a lot of people, so there was no sex, no violence, no bad language and no blood. 'That's the way they did it on the TV shows and it fits perfectly with us, taking a familiar genre and sending it up,' he said.

One major problem though was the time over-run. The first rough cut ran for more than two hours 30 minutes: 'terribly long,' commented Donner. 'We couldn't really have more than two hours,' so he and Gibson cut the first thirty minutes of the original film and shot some extra scenes for a revised beginning. Sadly, the need to cut ruthlessly meant that Linda Hunt, the diminutive actress who had been such a success with Gibson in *The Year of Living Dangerously* (1983), was taken out altogether.

'I loved the Linda Hunt sequence when I first read the script,' remembered Donner.

> She played a magician who saves Maverick from a hangman's noose, nurses him back to health, and gives him money to enter the poker game. It dealt with soul-searching, what life meant to him, his mother and his passion for cards. Linda is a wonderful actress and I loved the result, but when we edited everything together it didn't seem to work with the rest of the film. You cut what doesn't need to be there. You need to be ruthless, but it broke my heart to tell Linda.

Another notable feature of *Maverick* was the degree of ad libbing that went on. Explained Gibson: 'Richard (Donner) knows what he is doing and gives you a lot of freedom. We always played fast and loose with the *Lethal Weapon* scripts and I think it really works that way.'

The cast improvised to such a great extent, that concerns were expressed about the possible reaction of writer William Goldman. According to Gibson, however, he loved the final result. 'The script isn't carved in concrete and a good writer like Goldman is wise enough to know that he gave us a really good blueprint with which we could work,' explained Mel.

Once filming ended, Gibson did not spend long contemplating *Maverick*. The actor was now a choice piece of Hollywood property, among the biggest earners and the most sought-after.

The film opened in Britain in July 1994, just a month before he began work on the Scottish epic, *Braveheart*.

14 Braveheart Bonanza

Randall Wallace is an American, born in Tennessee, and a graduate of Duke University. With ambitions to be a writer he moved to Los Angeles, and later, with four novels to his credit, began writing for American television. Some months later he became a producer for Stephen Cannell Productions. At this point Randall Wallace was totally unknown to Mel Gibson.

The first fortuitous steps that would bring them together were taken when Wallace and his wife travelled to Scotland on vacation. On a visit to Edinburgh Castle he was impressed by an imposing statue guarding the castle gates. He was intrigued when he discovered that the statue represented William Wallace, not only because he and the great Scottish hero shared the same surname, but through the vague recollection that his own ancestors came from Scotland or Ireland and that he might just be related in some way. Being a professional writer and naturally inquisitive, he delved into the background of William Wallace and the extraordinary legends that have since come to mean so much to the people of Scotland.

But the American discovered that, legends apart, very few solid facts were known about him. So he began reading a 1740 English translation of rhyming Scottish verse presenting legends about Wallace. He started to formulate some personal views and impressions. 'History is impressionistic,' he explained. 'What William Wallace did can be inferred from the passion of his supporters and the hatred of his enemies. The great legends built a fire in my heart. His life communicated that you will prevail if you are faithful to what you believe in, and if those you love believe in you. Your body can be broken, but not your spirit.'

166

He still wondered, not too seriously perhaps, if he might be a descendant of William Wallace. Whether or not he was distantly related, the writer certainly felt some affinity of spirit with the great Scottish legend now. As a Hollywood screenwriter, that was enough for him to see the possibilities of putting William Wallace on film. The prospect filled him with enthusiasm and he returned to Scotland to continue his research into the Scottish patriot's 700-year-old story. Back in the United States he set about the detailed and painstaking business of piecing together a coherent account of this fabulous piece of history.

The next, and only remaining, piece in the jigsaw goes back to the early days of Hollywood in the 1940s. Alan Ladd, then a famous leading man, had died prematurely when only fifty-one, but not before he had fathered Alan Ladd Jnr, who, many years later, became a famous film executive in Hollywood. It was while he was with MGM that a script came into his hands which he felt had enormous possibilities. When he left MGM to re-establish his The Ladd Company at Paramount in 1993, he was able to take the script with him, bringing it to the attention of Mel Gibson and his associates at Icon Productions, Bruce Davey and Stephen McEveety.

Gibson recalled that particular moment: 'I couldn't wait to turn each page and was surprised at every turn. The screenplay had everything – heroic battles, a powerful love story and the passion of one man's strength which fires a whole country against its aggressors.' It was, of course, the screenplay written by Randall Wallace – the same screenplay which would become the basis of a hugely successful film, and at the same time, signal a significant advance in the already formidable career of Mel Gibson.

The film was *Braveheart*. Icon Productions secured the backing of Paramount Pictures and 20th Century Fox, but Gibson's own commitment was crucial. He would not only play the leading role, but take over as director and co-producer, the latter along with Alan Ladd Jnr and Bruce Davey, in a punishing year-long schedule. It was possibly the most exciting project any of them had so far undertaken, a big-scale spectacular drama with a massive cast and elaborate set pieces. Explained Gibson: 'William Wallace is one of the people who have changed the course of history. His is an incredible story about courage, loy-

167

alty, honour and the brutality of war. The film is also an inspiring love story.' When the film was completed Gibson seemed pleased with what he had accomplished. He commented: 'To the telling of this story I've devoted more than a year of my life – every minute has been worth it.'

William Wallace is arguably the greatest hero of the Scottish people. His legend inspired 100,000 people to gather on 24 June 1861 – some 556 years after his death – at the opening ceremony of the 300-foot National Monument in Stirling that still stands to honour his memory. It was here that Wallace once led a band of desperate and outnumbered Scots to a glorious victory over the English. The fabled five-foot sword that once belonged to Wallace is on display in Stirling Castle.

Born around the year 1267, Wallace was the second son of a middle-class landowner and was educated at Paisley Abbey by his uncle. Material wealth was of no concern to Wallace, who refused the Crown of Scotland when it was offered to him. While the Scottish nobles around him were accepting lands and titles from the English king Edward I, Wallace remained committed to the freedom and honour of Scotland. William Wallace, Braveheart, was a man of his times, a period that is familiar to few, but which has contributed many of the most enduring and familiar images of the Middle Ages. It was an age stained by cruelty and violence, yet also a splendid and heroic time when the ideal of freedom was first beginning to thrive.

Screenwriter Randall Wallace believed his screenplay for *Braveheart* captured the spirit of William Wallace. But the entire process of converting Wallace to the screen was a story of commitment, dedication and courage almost as intense and impressive as the hero's own inspirational life.

The logistics were immense. For scenes of the savage battles of Stirling and Falkirk, for example, some 1,700 troops were used, along with hundreds of extras. All the battle scenes were carefully choreographed to ensure everyone's safety. Mechanical and real horses, as many as 150 of the latter, were used, recruited from riding centres all around Ireland, and including twenty-five comprising a specially trained team from a well-known stables in Wokingham, Berkshire. It was Tony Smart, head of the stables, who guided Gibson through a scene in which he gallops up the stone steps of York Castle and batters down a door with his horse's front hooves before jumping forty feet into the moat below. 'He rides well and is a good listener,' observed Tony. The two mechanical horses, designed by special effects supervisor Nick Allder, were used in some of the more dangerous and spectacular stunts. Each horse, mounted on a stretch of track, could be accelerated from zero to 30 m.p.h. (50 k.p.h.) in a mere twenty-foot stretch. Reaching the end of the track a piston automatically kicked in between the back legs of the horse, causing the 'animal' to perform a spectacular somersault.

Altogether two dozen stunt experts were used in making the film, working under two stunt co-ordinators. They put the film extras through an intensive two weeks of training before shooting began. Gibson wanted to add an almost documentary feel to the battle scenes. He had a specific vision of the film, particularly the battle scenes. 'You watch *Spartacus* and after a couple of shots it turns into chaos,' he explained. 'I wanted to do something more than slash and gash . . . I wanted to tell a story.' A complete village, representing Lanark, was built in seven weeks. More than 6,000 costumes were designed by specialist Charles Knode. Some 10,000 arrows were used.

On-site preparations for *Braveheart* began ten weeks prior to five months of principal photography in Scotland and Ireland in 1994. Filming began in Scotland at the base of Ben Nevis, Britain's highest mountain, on 6 June. The Glen Nevis valley provided a majestic setting for the village of Lanark, where William Wallace lived as a child. It was there, some years later and on his return to the village as an adult, that he fell in love with Murron. There had been an innocent attraction between them even as children.

Glen Nevis has the highest rainfall in Europe, and for the six-week shoot in Scotland it rained almost non-stop, as expected. The important wedding scene was slotted in during the only three days of sunshine during the whole of this period of filming. Most of *Braveheart*, however, was shot in Ireland, mainly because of that country's generous system of tax incentives for film-makers, though Gibson claimed that the decision to shoot in Ireland was purely creative. 'We couldn't find battlefields and locations in the UK to make it cost-effective for us,' he explained. 'In fact the actual move to go over there will use up

169

any incentive that we gain, so we're no better off budgetary-wise,' he explained at the time.

But the location was never remotely in doubt once the Irish arts minister agreed, as part of the deal, to provide 1,700 members of the Irish Reserve army for use as extras. These forces acted as the infantry, archery and cavalry divisions of the Scottish and English armies during the ferocious battles of Stirling and Falkirk, which were actually filmed on the Curragh and Ballymore Eustace private land. Twelve weeks of building, painting and plastering transformed the exterior of Trim Castle into the fortified English town of York, once seven-ton gates had been added and wooden buttresses replaced. On the other side of the massive wall, a London square was created, while Dunsoghly Castle doubled for the exterior of the film's Edinburgh Castle. A number of other locations in Ireland were used, along with the actual council chamber in Edinburgh (for a scene set in Mornay's castle). Most of the close-up scenes and some exterior sets were filmed at the Ardmore Studios, near Dublin.

Gibson set himself a prodigious task, doing what he said he would never do again after *The Man Without a Face*, that is, to act in and direct the same movie. He said that particular earlier experience had taken its toll at the time. 'It was as if your head was about to fly off your shoulders,' he gasped. And this time around, also, he had accepted that third responsibility, as co-producer. The starring role in itself was physically demanding and emotionally draining, requiring an astonishing range from sensitive and intimate moments to epic explosions of intense rage. The athleticism required – horse riding, hand-to-hand fighting, sprinting and so on – was in itself a challenge, and Gibson admitted to feeling the strain of it all.

This feeling was doubtless compounded by his decision once again to quit smoking, at least for the duration of the movie. For a forty-a-day smoker over many years, it was a difficult decision to make, but, according to colleagues on the set, he kept his resolve so far as they could judge, only lapsing when filming was over and he was in London working in darkened rooms on the sound mix. By this time he was probably feeling all of his thirty-nine years and one could perhaps understand, if the rumours were reliable, that he had at first turned down the role of

Wallace because he felt he was too old for the part. 'At first all I wanted to do was direct the picture,' he explained. But when he tried to finance the project, he found he could raise the money only if he agreed to take the starring role.

But the project held so much promise that Gibson was probably more exhilarated at the prospect of doing *Braveheart* than he had been for any of his other films. 'I've been sitting on the script for two years,' he explained at the time. 'When I first read Randy's script something about it haunted me, it had a great heart. Randy's great gift as a writer is that he is passionate and genuine.' Mel and Bruce Davey sat down with Randy Wallace over a period of several months, working on Wallace's original script. Gibson explained: 'It is an heroic story falling somewhere between fact and legend and in the end, and against such enormous odds of might and deceit, it was inevitable that Wallace failed.'

Braveheart is a story of passion, told with passion. Gibson spends the entire film dressed in rags, kilt riding up his legs, hair tumbling around his shoulders, and all the time facing the most appalling, life-threatening situations. These are the horrific events, set against impressive panoramas of marching armies, soldiers storming the battlements, with broadswords and realistic, vivid hand-to-hand battles, that turn him from a peaceful farmer into a bloodthirsty warrior.

There were lots of opportunities to tinker with the story and, certainly, some dramatic licence was used. 'When history got in the way of making a good film, we sort of bent it to our own devices,' explained Gibson, and as Randall Wallace pointed out: 'I'm a dramatist, not an historian.' Gibson admits that factual research and information was sketchy, but enough hard facts existed to suggest that Wallace should be more than merely a footnote in history. 'People have been known to kneel down and pray, for God's sake, when his name is mentioned.'

Gibson gave the picture substance, depth and, most of all, a compelling credibility because of his decision to take a strong and honest line. Brutal scenes are realistically played, but give not the slightest impression that they have been included gratuitously. The pathos is heart-rending when the lovely and sincere Murron, the one true love of Wallace's life, is murdered by having her throat slashed. And when the time comes for Wallace

171

himself to meet his fate, we sit through the desperate anguish, not just of his death, but through the excruciating stages of his being hanged, drawn and quartered by Edward and his followers. 'There was going to be no happy Hollywood ending,' Gibson warned quite early on, before going on to explain that the basic tone of the film was romantic, no matter how brutal it gets. 'Wallace never loses his love of his country and his freedom.' He said he did not, however, want to shy away from the brutality 'because it must have been hellish'.

And the picture certainly has its romantic and lighter moments. The love scenes between Gibson and Catherine McCormack, as Murron, and later between Gibson and the beautiful French star, Sophie Marceau, starring as the Princess Isabelle, are gentle and deeply sensitive. Who, moreover, could fail to raise a titter when, during battle, Wallace's troops, to a man, drop their trousers (or rather, hitch up their kilts!) as a collective and metaphoric two-fingers to the enemy. The essentially long and torrid story however, was kept in check by the disciplined script: few questions remained unanswered at the end.

At the time Gibson gave a fascinating insight into his approach to film-making. He explained that he shot the film mentally three times before deciding to direct it. The sheer scale of the picture, with its elaborate set pieces and spectacular action sequences involving upwards of 3,000 people, was an enormous undertaking compared with his only previous role as a director, in *The Man Without a Face*, with its simple story and few characters. But by the time the crew were on location and ready for work he had most of the film planned.

He had already done much background research on Wallace, his times and the areas in which he operated. He reviewed legends and poems to help get into the character and talked to author Andrew Fisher who, Gibson explained, was probably about the most unbiased and honest of all historians in his hypothesis of what might have happened. He also studied the military strategy of ancient battles and watched a lot of war films. He supposedly plotted much of the detail of some of the most vivid and realistic battle scenes ever committed to film by shifting toy soldiers around a table. 'But the character of Wallace was pretty much explained in the script,' he revealed, though in the end much of the triumph of *Braveheart* was down to intangibles such as atmosphere, tension, sensitivity and a feeling for period detail.

The way the action is selectively captured in slow-motion sequences both heightens the tension and allows the viewer to see, even explore the action; while by no means an original device, this technique is used intelligently and with restraint. Gibson said he wanted the film to look realistic, to be gritty and dirty. 'I didn't want it to look too Hollywood, too bright and colourful. I wanted *Braveheart* to reflect the times as much as possible.'

Here, nature came to his aid. He kept the cameras turning when the clouds drifted over, in the rain and hail. 'Sometimes it looks miserable, and it is,' he said. But for a story which Gibson once flippantly called 'skullduggery and double-dealing' the gloom often made the film's atmosphere seem somehow more medieval.

Despite the enormous pressures on Gibson, he would later reveal that the only times he ever has misgivings about directing or acting are before all the work begins. Then, smiling: 'Once you're in you need too much energy to throw it away. It's a lot of hard work, though I enjoy being involved up to the eyeballs.'

As director, Gibson would begin every day with what seemed like a million decisions to be taken. 'It was like doing a juggling act,' he revealed. One particular scene in a grassy wood involved him on camera. When his veteran English first assistant director David Tomblin shouted 'Action!' and then 'Cut!', Gibson rushed down the hillock to watch the scene replay on a monitor. It was his decision alone whether a take should be printed, his eye for detail meant that the scene would be shot repeatedly until he was satisfied. That kind of switching from actor to director, director to actor was commonplace for Gibson in *Braveheart*, because he is crucial to so many of the scenes on camera. And if that were not enough, he told a journalist that at night, after seeing the rushes of *Braveheart* in the editing suite in a distillery at Fort William, he would turn producer, viewing more rushes of another Icon film shooting in Prague, called *Immortal Beloved* starring Gary Oldman as Beethoven. It all made for a long day, explained a tired Gibson, adding that the key to it all was preparation, so that all the incidentals get in the way as little as possible.

173

But according to those around him, he seldom showed the strain he was under, breaking up tensions and fatigue with one of his pranks, an appalling joke or a simple touch of understanding. McCormack said that a lot of stink bombs and whoopee cushions were secreted abut the set. Marceau recalled the time when she said her lines and, not really happy with what she had done, turned to Gibson and enquired: 'Wasn't that too mush-mouthed?' 'Nah, it was great,' said Gibson. 'I'm making coffee. Anyone want some?'

More seriously, he conceded that he felt close to a nervous breakdown by the end of the film. 'I didn't fly off the handle much, but I was acting kind of strange for a while.' This was not altogether surprising, perhaps, since he also had to cope with a good deal of local public interest. In fact, making the film had created a sensation locally and even when some of the battle scenes were shot at night, and in the pouring rain, a large crowd of spectators would gather to catch a glimpse of the proceedings. The weather was foul, but the lucky onlookers would witness the remarkable sight of Mel Gibson, the warrior actor, with hair extensions enclosed in a plastic bag and protected by a bush hat, directing operations and very much master of his own destiny. He would set up a shot, then leap in front of the camera for a couple of takes. At other times he would be huddled under a huge umbrella to escape the rain and then would be seen striding energetically through the mud to check on this, to advise that, and generally keep a close eye on things.

Gibson *was* Braveheart. He himself wrote the inspired scene of a priest praying with the soldiers before battle – he felt these guys (priests) would have been around and battlefield absolutions were pretty common in those days.

In shooting an epic biopic like *Braveheart* with such vast numbers of people involved and so much at stake, it is customary for tensions to be quietly bubbling just beneath the surface. But by all accounts Gibson ran what is known in the business as a 'contented shoot'. Communication, explained Gibson, was the key. 'If you don't get the message to everyone all along the line, it's chaos. It's really a question of everyone being in touch and knowing what's expected of them. Then the director is simply a marshalling voice when needed.' It appears that Gibson was his customarily democratic self on the set. You would find him queuing at the trailer for his food along with the rest of the crew. He was one of the team and did not expect, or receive, any special treatment.

The basic story of *Braveheart* is easily assimilated. Sometime during the late thirteenth century, William Wallace (Gibson) returns to Scotland after living away from his homeland for some years. The king of Scotland has died without an heir and the king of England, a ruthless despot known as Edward the Longshanks (because of his height), has seized the throne. Wallace becomes the leader of a ramshackle yet courageous army determined to vanquish the greater English forces.

Wallace's courage and passion for his country unite his people behind him and, driven by anger and grief after the brutal murder of his new, young bride, he resolves to avenge her death and to fight on for Scotland's freedom. At the battle of Stirling, Wallace leads his army to a stunning victory and, knighted by the grateful Scottish nobles, Sir William Wallace extends the conflict south of the border, storming the city of York. Unable to rely on his ineffectual son, Prince Edward, Longshanks sends his daughter-in-law, Princess Isabelle, to discuss a truce with Wallace. But the inspired Wallace continues his crusade until, after monumental battles, intrigue and deception, personal vendetta and betrayal, he pays the ultimate price.

A remarkable feature about *Braveheart* was that at almost every turn the project looked to be an extraordinary risk. Some twenty months before release, its future looked bleak, in the relentless drizzle of a remote Scottish mountainside. That it became such an outstanding success, artistically and commercially, is largely due to the comprehensive commitment and self-belief of Mel Gibson. Even the cast list included no other heavyweight to pull in the crowds. Gibson somehow did it on his own.

By chance or design – Gibson claims he simply chose the actors who just seemed to him to fit the characters best – *Braveheart* ended up with a cast of virtual unknowns. The then 23-year-old Catherine McCormack was an out-of-work actress at the time but, as one crew member detected, 'possessed a smile that could fell any man at twenty paces.' Though of Scottish ancestry, McCormack was born and raised in Alton, Hampshire, and trained at the Oxford School of Drama.

Equally well cast and just as lissome – but no better known in

Britain – was Sophie Marceau, whose appearance in *Braveheart* marked her starring début in an English language film. Twenty-eight when she made *Braveheart*, the French-born actress has a cool, elegant beauty. She gained widespread recognition in the hit film *La Boum*, and for *La Boum 2* she received a César award for 'female revelation of the year'.

'She's a very particular young woman,' says Gibson. 'She looks like royalty and she behaves that way too; very regal and statuesque.' Mel Gibson, always his own man, demonstrated a novel approach to casting. It seems he dispensed with any reading of the parts when auditioning. He simply chatted individually with McCormack and Marceau for a while, just getting to know them, and made up his mind on that basis. At an international press conference organized by 20th Century Fox at the Hotel du Cap in Antibes Gibson announced that Sophie Marceau would play Isabelle. 'We just spoke in London for about two hours,' he explained. 'She immediately understood what the role was about and I didn't think it necessary for her to do a screen test.'

The role of King Edward I also proved a shrewd piece of casting – again it was conducted by Gibson with a similar neglect of convention. Patrick McGoohan had a long and distinguished acting pedigree in films, on the stage and television particularly, with ninety-six episodes of *Danger Man* (*Secret Agent* in the US) and *The Prisoner* to his credit. Gibson regarded the suggestion by first assistant director David Tomblin, a good friend of McGoohan, that he would be ideal in the part, as an inspired move. He was a brilliant choice as the inscrutable, ruthless Longshanks. Said Gibson: 'When I met Patrick I knew he just had to be the king. He was tall enough and he had this intense concentration. His nose was a bit small, so we sculpted a fake nose for him to use.'

Angus McFadyen, as Robert the Bruce, turned in a particularly memorable performance in his motion picture debut. Robert the Bruce pledges support to Wallace but, along with the Scottish nobles, quits the field with their cavalry at the battle of Falkirk, leaving Wallace's infantry exposed. The Bruce, however, is a reluctant ally of the English and helps Wallace to escape. Some years later, though not fully covered in the film, Robert the Bruce, having decided to oppose the English once and for all, invokes Wallace's name on the field of Bannockburn with a victory that would establish the independence of Scotland.

How many filmgoers, it might be wondered, took note that the down-cast role of Stewart was played by Donal Gibson, younger brother of Mel? But Gibson fans, and many critics too, would rush to tell you that the shrewdest casting of all was to give himself the starring role. Said writer Ian Nathan: 'What is so evident among *Braveheart*'s earthy hugeness is Gibson's self-belief. As actor he is majestic – his looks extended to a mighty hazel mane, his Hollywood good looks set like the face of Ben Nevis, his highland accent surprisingly authentic – fearlessly accessing the man's consuming battle frenzy as much as his growing heroism.' Certainly, by widespread acclaim, he produced a convincing and authentic Wallace, using hair extensions and face paint to get the warrior's appearance right. 'The rest was just mud and dirt,' added Gibson.

From the start *Braveheart* was a picture Mel Gibson was desperate to do. 'It's like all the big movies I grew up with as a kid ... *The Vikings, Spartacus*,' he explained. He was anxious to prove his directorial skills, but knew his professional reputation would be on the line. He still recalled the raised eyebrows and the pained expressions when he had dared to play *Hamlet*. In taking on *Braveheart* he realized he had to make it work.

Financially, the film was difficult to get off the ground. Reports suggested that Alan Ladd Jnr had originally indicated to Paramount that the cost of the movie would work out at about $40 million, but later estimates racked it up to almost half as much again. In the end Paramount, which was then going through change after being taken over by Viacom, committed $17.5 million for the US distribution rights; 20th Century Fox stepped in with $37 million for the foreign rights. Private investors were roped in and Gibson underlined his personal confidence in the project by advancing the production $15 million of his own money to keep things afloat while the studios sorted themselves out. He had already agreed to forgo a fee for starring in the picture until such a time as the studios had earned back their investments, including the cost of marketing and distribution. Other economies were made by Gibson. He cut one scene completely and saved money by rewriting it with much less dialogue, so it could be shot in just one day, saving two weeks of night shooting.

In spite of all manner of problems faced by Gibson in telling the stirring tale of Scotland's ancient freedom fighter, with huge armies in bloody combat, there was a remarkable degree of confidence in the outcome. Paramount, in fact, despite knowing that filming had not started until 6 June 1994, seemed so assured of its inevitable success that they moved in early to announce a tentative US release date for the picture: Memorial Day, 30 May 1995.

Whether Gibson shared such confidence is not known, for with filming at an end he faced the gigantic task of cutting close to one million feet of footage, about three times that of an average film. This was hardly surprising, for the legendary battle of Stirling between the British and the Scots alone took thirty days to shoot using ten cameras and involving 3,000 people. Gibson said that when he signed to direct the movie Paramount had insisted that it should run for no longer than two hours 15 minutes. 'When I showed them the rough cut it was three hours 40 minutes so we came to an agreement. They tore up the contract and I cut an hour out of the film.' And he commented with some pride: 'I brought the movie in for $53 million (£34 million) in just 105 days,' which was a remarkably short time for a picture of this scale and scope. Within a very short time of its American release *Braveheart* had grossed £40 million.

Braveheart was a classic Hollywood epic, though Gibson might balk at the comment, and undoubtedly one of the very best of its kind ever made. It was also the most expensive movie directed by an actor, one which turned out to be Paramount's blockbuster of the year. Yet when asked how he thought the reviews would turn out, he was at his modest and disarming best. 'I really worked hard on this one,' he said. 'Some people may love it; others may savage it, because you'll never be everybody's cup of tea. That's all there is to it.'

In fact it was hard to fault Gibson. His skills as an actor were well-enough known, but as a director he really had to prove himself. He certainly did that, in the most convincing and profound way, showing vision and understanding, together with a feeling for what would work and the ability and know-how to produce the results. One reviewer enthused:

178

He is passionate and controlled, harnessing the thousands of extras
to create the awesome in-yer-face battle scenes, free-flowing with
decapitatory and limb-lopping enthusiasm, while drawing sparkling
performances from his cast, be they mud-caked, kilt-lifting warriors
or preened maidens. The haunting loveliness of McCormack and the
silver-tongued grace of Marceau, add welcome softness to the furore.

Gibson's work on *Braveheart* earned him not only a critical
respect and a large audience, but also the unqualified admiration
of many of his contemporaries in the film business. Richard
Donner, who had directed Gibson in *Maverick* and the *Lethal
Weapon* films, and his wife were invited by Mel to the very first
showing of the uncut film. He said that it stretched to three and
a half hours, 'but I could very easily have taken another two
hours of that movie.' He said it was, first of all, epic. 'On top of
that, for him to have tackled that film – to play the lead role
would have been good enough; but to have directed it as well!
He's amazing. I don't think anything scares Mel.'

Despite rumours of battle-scarred extras – even some serious
injuries – no significant incidents were reported. 'There was one
broken ankle though and three hang-nails,' said Gibson. But he
failed to mention that he himself pulled a groin muscle trying to
mount a horse. Having his own chiropractor on the set helped
him cope with the eighteen-hour day. The rumours of injuries
probably arose after a particularly gruesome rough cut of the
film. Gibson said he wanted people to know what thirteenth-
century warfare was like. It was so realistic when he showed it
to some people in its original form that they ran out of the theatre. 'It was just too harsh,' he conceded. Then an amusing post-
script: 'With the new version people still think, whoa! but they
don't run out of the theatre!'

Reviewers gave it the thumbs-up. One enthused: 'Gibson has
exceeded the loftiest of expectations with a quite stunning piece
of film-making.' Another claimed it the 'greatest epic since
Lawrence of Arabia.' Reported *Flicks*: 'Not since the Sixties and
the heyday of films like *El Cid* and *Fall of the Roman Empire* has
there been an historical tale of such dazzling cinematic scope
and size.' Even so, the possibility of Gibson's creation totting up
an Oscar or two seemed optimistic in the extreme. Paramount
harboured few, if any, ambitions of that sort when the film
opened in the United States.

179

Then something extraordinary occurred. Audiences discovered some kind of magic in *Braveheart*. The film remained in American cinemas all through the summer, long after it might have been expected to have worn itself out. Paramount chiefs woke up one morning to realize they just might have a popular and a critical hit on their hands. Hurriedly, they gave the film an ambitious relaunch, with a record multi-million-dollar marketing strategy in the United States alone. In just fourteen weeks box-office takings in the United States had reached $80 million. In Europe and elsewhere receipts would soon reach $70 million. When *Braveheart* captured ten Oscar nominations, the studio chiefs again dipped into their corporate budgets to relaunch the picture for a second time.

Typical of the down-to-earth Mel Gibson, knowledgeable, deep-thinker, yet funny-man and practical joker as well, he received the phenomenal success of *Braveheart* as just another bonus in his job as a movie-maker, behind or in front of the camera. Characteristically modest about his success, he told a press conference: 'Producing and directing offer satisfaction, but you can't just grab it right away. You must establish a credit rating. We're getting there.' At a time of probably his greatest professional triumph he continued to be something of a reluctant hero.

While in Scotland Gibson had rented a mansion near Fort William and Robyn and the children, then aged four to fourteen, joined him for part of his stay in the Highlands. It was the home he had earlier occupied for six months while on pre-production work and when scouting for locations for *Braveheart*, his kids then going to the local state school. They spent some time with him on the set and, according to reports, the children could be seen at one time wandering around in the background dressed as thirteenth-century urchins.

An altogether more relaxed Mel Gibson finally celebrated the end of a rigorous bout of filming by having fun with his family at their Californian beach home. The 38-year-old Robyn watched happily as her husband romped with the children, laughing at their antics as they played on the beach, hunted crabs, built sand-castles, or raced screaming into the water.

The impact of *Braveheart* in Scotland, in particular, though not exclusively, was a modern movie phenomenon. Its influence stretched across broad sections of British life. From sport to nationalist politics, in public polls and awards, by groups of people and individuals, *Braveheart* was ubiquitous. Politicians and political journalists had a field day. Under the headline 'Battling over *Braveheart*', the *Guardian* reported that 'rival parties in Scotland are vying to grab the political pickings from Mel Gibson's new film'. In sport the *London Evening Standard*, in its pre-match reporting of the England-Scotland football clash at Wembley, quoted Manchester United's Scottish manager, Alex Ferguson: 'I hope Craig Brown [Scotland's manager] sits the players down and regales them with stirring stories of the past. Then he should put on the film *Braveheart* and get them raring to go at Wembley.' But football was not alone. Golf: 'Super-Scot ... marked her cup debut with a *Braveheart* display' (*BBC Ceefax*). Racing: 'Only the *Brave Hearts* will be jumping for joy' (*Daily Mail*).

Polls and awards reflected the saturation coverage of *Braveheart*. The Scottish *Daily Record* used a large photograph of Gibson in battledress with the heading: 'William Wallace voted Top Scot of all time' (Gavin Hastings was voted second, with less than half of Wallace's votes, then Stephen Hendry, Robert Burns and Alexander Fleming). The readers of *Empire* film magazine voted overwhelmingly for *Braveheart* as the Best Movie of 1995. So did the readers of *Flicks*. It was best action film of the year and also best film of the year on BBC Radio Five. It was one of Barry Norman's top ten films of the year. *Braveheart* was also voted Best Film by the general public and thus received the Lloyds Bank People's Award, presented at the BAFTA awards ceremony. Gibson's personal tally also included the Golden Globe Award for Best Director and Best Director at the Convention of the National Association of Theater Owners. After the Oscars he also received the American MTV Movie Award for Directing the Best Action Sequence.

In September 1997 a huge statue of William Wallace was unveiled in Stirling by Nigel Tranter, the historical novelist. Its creator, Tom Church, said he modelled the new statue on Mel Gibson. It was given a prominent position in a new £400,000 visitor complex built to cater for the surge of interest created by *Braveheart*. Thousands of extra visitors had been recorded since the 1995 film.

Braveheart? What's *Braveheart*? Yes, there still remains the vague feeling that Mel Gibson is the sort of person you just might need to remind from time to time that *Braveheart* was indeed a rather special film and earned him not just one, but two Oscars – for Best Picture (shared with Bruce Davey and Alan Ladd Jnr) and Best Director. And the picture itself scooped three more Oscars, as well as receiving nominations in five other categories.

15 'The Man's Magic!'

Someone once asked Mel Gibson if he had heard of William Wallace before getting involved with *Braveheart*. He responded instantly. 'Yeah, sure' he said. 'It's the name of a pub in Sydney.' Was this Mel playing the fool yet again? Or was he serious? The twinkling blue eyes do not always give the game away. You see, there did just happen to be a William Wallace Hotel on the out-skirts of Sydney; it may still be there today. It is this wide-eyed sense of innocence and humour which prompted *Vanity Fair* writer Stephen Schill to pronounce: 'It's partly Gibson's refusal to take acting seriously that makes him so good at it.' Mel says simply: 'I just generally like to horse around, you know.'

His tomfoolery knows no bounds and is mostly so infectious that it carries all before it. Just occasionally though, depending on his mood, it leaves behind a vapour trail of irritation, even anger, however unintended. For he can be blunt and coarse as well as funny. On the set of *Lethal Weapon 2* he added to his basic repertoire of painful puns, clowning antics and cleverly executed pratfalls by wearing coffee filters on his head and bel-lowing renditions of Edelweiss. Not to forget his strategically timed belches. He certainly knows how to enjoy himself and to cut through life's tensions. He loved doing *Hamlet* but, as some-one remarked at the time: 'He was a bit too dour for Mel to hang on to for long.'

When working on a film Gibson quickly steps in if he senses things are becoming a bit heavy. That's when you expect him to emerge wearing the red nose which he is supposed to keep handy in his pocket ready for a quick fix of fun. He admits to loving the ancient, innocent humour of the Three Stooges and his own jokes are mostly harmless and endearing.

He has a quick-response mechanism and his fun, from unlikely gestures to pained little-boy expressions, can be targeted at himself as well as others. When labelled with the notorious 'sexiest man alive' label his tongue-in-cheek response took his audience by surprise. 'That implies there are a lot of dead guys who got more points than I did.' When a photographer was trying to pose him decorously by a poolside, he waited a second or two, then quipped: 'How about if I just walk on the water?'

Mind you, Gibson's jokes can sometimes border on the dubious if not actually crude or in bad taste and, when driven by impulse and little else, are not always welcome or appreciated. In his latest film, *Conspiracy Theory*, he surely went too far. He allegedly sent co-star Julia Roberts a beautifully wrapped gift parcel. When she opened it she is said to have come face to face with a dead rat. Perhaps he should have put on his red nose instead! But Roberts forgave him in the end. It seems that her dazzlingly famous smile had been lacking as she struggled to recover from a failed relationship and some spiteful drubbing from the notorious Hollywood machine. Gibson had noticed and took action. But once she overcame the shock, his woeful joke was seen to be just what the doctor ordered, and enough to have Roberts smiling again in no time. It was rumoured that he kept a similar freeze-dried rat handy to ward off pushy autograph hunters.

Against all this evidence it is hard to believe those closest to Gibson, who maintain that his joking is often no more than a defence mechanism, a means of keeping certain situations or aspects of life at arm's length. Yet he has been a funny man most of his life. In some of the less absurd scenes from *Maverick*, for instance, one can easily detect that sense of the mischievous, innocent, even vulnerable Mel Gibson lurking behind the action.

The mantle of fame and the trappings of stardom rest uneasily on Gibson's shoulders. He is not part of the Hollywood set and is seldom seen at receptions and glitzy parties; the superficial gloss of film-making carries little meaning for him. He once said that Hollywood, like fame, success and failure, is something you have to come to terms with. This statement clearly suggests a feet-on-the-ground, down-to-earth character, one who is unwilling to be sucked in by the mesmeric ways of Hollywood.

He seems to have devised his own way of balancing the extremes of life as a global superstar.

He does not deny that he enjoys being fabulously wealthy, yet at the same time gives no indication that, having acquired life-long security for himself and his family, he indulges in wholesale excess for the sake of it. Nor has prosperity diminished his affection for, and his deep loyalty towards, the fundamentals of his trade. The process of film-making has lost none of its attraction or meaning over the years.

His natural and evident assets as a film star can be summarized as 'wholesome'. Instantly, you take him to be pleasant, good-natured, with an easy outgoing personality. His stunning good looks somehow appear accessible and he seems friendly and open, not brooding or mysterious like Richard Gere, for instance, or difficult to fathom like Tom Cruise. Yet he has never fully capitalized on his strong box-office appeal. Rather, he pursues his art with a keen *personal* ambition – always eager to test himself and extend his horizons.

Few major stars have put their reputations on the line in quite the way Gibson has, with an enormously wide range of roles that have stretched his repertoire as an actor. Unlike some top stars, he seems to value the integrity of his career, choosing his films with great care. Those who work with him closely testify to his high professional standards. He goes for good stories, competent scripts and he thinks seriously about what he is doing and where he is going. His intelligence, ambition to do a good job and his attitude make a significant contribution to the process of film-making. His movies, though many and varied, are anything but superficial – though Gibson would be the first to admit, possibly with a couple of mild expletives thrown in, that they did not all work out as he expected and that some were definitely much worse than others.

He does not give the impression that he is above the system and curiously, while being one of Hollywood's biggest earners, still maintains an air of being largely non-commercial outside films. He shows little interest in exploiting his name and position commercially, except in areas which interest him. He did a couple of recordings, reading *My Cousin Rachel* in 1986 and *David and Goliath* about ten years later. The latter, in particular, was praised. When he flexed his vocal cords as the heroic

185

Englishman Captain Smith in Disney's more recent cartoon film, *Pocahontas*, Gibson enjoyed the experience, but again felt obliged to lighten things up. 'I just hope there isn't going to be a concert tour,' he joked. Director Mike Gabriel said: 'He did it for his six kids.'

Whilst by no means a cynic, Mel Gibson does have another, harder side. No one reaches his exalted status by being easygoing, fun-loving and everybody's friend all the time – especially in the killing field of Hollywood. Gibson can be as difficult as the next person. When under pressure, for example when his private life is under threat or he is being given a rough time by the press, his anger spills over with a few choice words; even a walk-out. One notable occasion was an MTV Movie awards ceremony which he attended to receive a presentation. Reports suggested he left the premises in a fit of rage after being surprised by an unrehearsed backstage interview, which, unknown to Gibson, was being broadcast elsewhere in the building.

His co-stars are in close enough contact with him over a long enough time for their opinions to count. Mostly, they praise him highly, particularly at a professional level. But it is no secret that Julia Roberts found him at times 'difficult' and Helena Bonham-Carter didn't quite know what to make of him, though after playing Ophelia to his *Hamlet*, she could understand his complexities 'what with the Catholicism, the Australian bit and all those Irish strands'. She also said his humour could be a bit lavatorial.

But most of his co-stars are likely to line up alongside Patsy Kensit in acknowledging the professional value in working with Gibson. 'I learned a lot from working with him on *Lethal Weapon 2*,' she said. 'He's a brilliant actor and improvises all the time. He taught me that you don't have to "perform" a character. It's just the way you say, for example, "Pass me a glass of water" or whatever, that reveals all about you.'

'There's an honesty about him which sometimes scares people,' said *Ransom* co-star Rene Russo. Sigourney Weaver said he doesn't like being the subject of scrutiny and 'he can sing and dance and he's all over the place and is very funny'. Commented Goldie Hawn: 'He's very attractive and very sexy.' Sophie Marceau said: 'He's a great seducer'; Jodie Foster: 'He's like your best buddy'; and Diane Keaton: 'Oh my God, the man's magic.'

His impatience with the press, his contempt for their efforts to probe into his private life, are almost legendary. On one notable occasion he became so angry about some unauthorized biography that he swore if he ever met the author he would 'tear his face right off'.

For all his easy-going chumminess, Gibson is likely to admit that he is not so brimful of virtue as a cursory glance might suggest. You need to probe behind that cheeky, innocent smile to discover the real Mel, who has strong views on many aspects of life and is forthright in expressing them, even when they may appear irrational to many people. Take the violence, even brutality, in many of his films. 'Subscribing to the theory that people are affected by film violence is bullshit,' he countered when a journalist tackled him on the possibility of *Ransom* promoting violence.

Gibson's earlier years threw up stories about his boozing and womanizing, and he has spoken frankly about the past: 'I drank a lot and thumped people. My emotions bothered me. Self-destructiveness is there in all of us.' Having long since emerged from his dark days and with his drinking now under control, he can still joke about it. He told one journalist that he directed and starred in *Braveheart* after passing out in a New Jersey bar and woke up to find himself wearing a kilt and blue face paint. And about the more sensational stories that have gone the rounds over the years? Mel's answer was not unexpected: 'I'm vindictive and when someone lies about me in the press I want to kill them, but nowadays I just don't give a damn what people write about me.' Mel's director on all three *Lethal Weapon*s, Richard Donner, has Gibson figured. 'Under the good-looking facade, he's a real tough son-of-a-bitch,' he said. 'Though widely considered, a decent sort of guy,' said one close observer, 'you cross him at your peril – even just once.'

Gibson continues to be an inveterate, if intermittent smoker, despite his numerous efforts to give up the habit. He agrees moodily that it is not a good example for his children, but his devotion to his family is an example often quoted in Hollywood and cannot be doubted. Almost all of his time from work is spent with his family. His kids include him in their plans and when they were younger, he would be roped in to play their games. He once said: 'I'm as big a kid as they are; they think I'm one of them.' He maintains contact with his brothers and sisters and has always kept in close touch with his father. He continues to mourn the death of his mother. He remains a committed, devout Catholic, even if these days worship is less formal, structured and dogmatic than that of his youth.

One important facet easily overlooked, beneath the light-hearted, joky persona, is the deeper aspect of his character. For a start, he is extremely intelligent, well-read, articulate and a deep and honest thinker. He is much smarter than he likes to appear and is resolute when it comes to the business of making films. The way he approaches and handles a role, how he cleverly steers a film through inevitable hazards from the director's chair, are valid testimony to his skills, abilities and instincts. Don't be fooled by the way he moves in and out of serious talk, baring his soul one minute, joking the next. Someone revealed a hint of the deeper Gibson when they said he treats being called the sexiest man alive like an affliction. Richard Donner, director of some of his most successful movies and someone who knows Gibson better than most, says his gift for language is not immediately apparent to the outside world, 'yet he is one of the best-read, most well-versed men I've ever met. His command and love of the English language are phenomenal.'

'He is also unpretentious to the point of self-effacement,' declared an associate in 1995, trying to explore the hidden side of Gibson. 'There is no stir when he enters a room – usually because he has arrived via the side door, brought no entourage and, in wrinkled blue polo shirt, jeans and sneakers, doesn't look like a screen idol at all.' In short, he is a complicated mixture of superficiality and depth, with a dark side to his character.

His physical stature helps his anonymity in a crowd. At about 5 feet 9 inches tall and a little over 11 stones these days, he has never rushed to bare his torso in films. 'I really try to keep my clothes on these days,' he explained frivolously, 'in case anyone might just jump to the wrong conclusion.' Curiously, for all his fame, he has never been a role model. One analysis of Gibson's popularity suggests that being relatively short and slight for the old style traditional hero, he does not overwhelm or threaten. 'Men can see him as a pal, women someone whom they can protect and who needs them.' Anyone searching for the real Mel Gibson receives little help. He normally offers few clues. He counters questions on this particular subject with statements like: 'People are looking for some hidden meanings, but there are none.' Indeed, what you see is what you get.

He is also incredibly committed to his chosen profession of movie actor and, now, director. He is certainly keen to do more directing and explained his feelings like this: 'Writers like Towne, doctors like Miller, become directors, but what they and others all have in common is a desire and need to tell a story. That is what you are doing as an actor. But only as a director do you have all the tools at your disposal.' Asked if he was ambitious, he replied: 'Yeah, but the only ambition I have is to do a good job . . .'

Seldom is there a time when one project or another is not occupying at least some part of his mind. After the enormous worldwide triumph of *Braveheart*, some actors might have rested on their laurels, wondering where the next blockbuster was coming from. Gibson was refreshingly philosophical, his attitude being that *Braveheart* was just one in a number of movies he would make. It just happened to be a huge success. So what if the next one doesn't turn out to be as big? The implication is that life goes on, success or failure, and as a professional movie actor there is always a new movie to be considered, a decision to be made. He told a reporter at about this time: 'The most important thing is to live in the present. People don't stay in the present enough.' He said that people get 'too steamed up about the past and kind of worry too much about the future'. Mind you, there was little for Gibson to worry about as he signed up with Disney to make a $61 million blockbuster, for a fee (and a healthy percentage of the receipts) which fully reflected his substantial power-rating in Hollywood. He was reportedly the first actor to receive an estimated $24 million for a project.

After *Braveheart* Gibson would unwittingly take his cue from the devotion he feels for his own family. Respected Hollywood director Ron Howard was the conduit. Howard had succeeded recently and conspicuously with the double-Oscar-winning *Apollo 13*, starring Tom Hanks and Gary Sinise, for which he was named Best Director of the Year by the Directors Guild of America. When he came across a script by Richard Price and Alexander Ignon he knew he had found his next project. And when that same script eventually arrived at Gibson's door the story touched a highly sensitive nerve. For he found that the screenplay was about the kidnapping of a much-loved young son and its aftermath.

It stopped Gibson in his tracks. He went through mental torture as he thought about the possibilities of one of his own children being abducted. It wasn't an unusual phenomenon. It was happening all the time in the United States, and successful people, Hollywood celebrities among them, were seen as being particularly vulnerable. Gibson was hooked. He explained later: 'If you're a parent, it's your worst nightmare – that's the pull of the film.'

Ransom began production in New York in January 1996, avoiding the city's snowiest winter on record by filming on sound stages in the district of Queens, during the first two months of production. Gibson, who reportedly secured the lead after Howard had considered Harrison Ford and Tom Cruise, plays Tom Mullen, a self-made, publicity-conscious and wealthy corporate executive, the millionaire boss of his own airline and one who is experienced in mediating tough business deals. He oozes his way through life possessing all the material trappings of high success, including a luxurious Fifth Avenue penthouse, an enviable position in New York society and what is known in the jargon as 'high media visibility'. He has a beautiful wife, Kate (played by Rene Russo), and a young son Sean (the ten-year-old Brawley Nolte, son of Nick Nolte), whom his parents adore.

The self-assured tycoon's position and stretch-limo lifestyle appear impregnable until young Sean goes missing while attending a science fair in Central Park. Tom's world of affluence and privilege comes crashing down once he knows that Sean has been abducted by desperate criminals and is being held for ransom. The price for his freedom? Just $2 million.

Once over the immediate shock, Tom's gut reaction is to meet the kidnappers' demands and simply pay the bill for his son's release. But the FBI steps in to concoct an ingenious plot which will not only save paying out the $2 million, which they cannot condone, but will enable them to catch the kidnappers. When the drop-off they organize goes wrong, a man ends up dead and the child stays kidnapped. It is then that Tom's resolve stiffens. Now he is not just worried, but very angry. His instincts as a tough business operator have always warned him against simply handing over the ransom without any guarantee of his son's safety. He now believes that, even if he did, the kidnappers might well find it too dangerous to let his boy go. When he becomes convinced that the kidnappers do not intend to return his son alive, he resolves not to pay the $2 million. Instead he appears on prime-time television to announce that he is to double the $2 million ransom, but is now offering the money as a reward to anyone who brings in the kidnappers, dead or alive.

It is a monumental gamble which not only places his own life at risk, but terrifies his wife, putting her love for him and her safety in jeopardy, and sets the police against him. Most of all there is the risk that the kidnappers will become so incensed and frustrated at seeing their hoped-for $2 million disappear that they will take their revenge by killing the boy before taking flight. It's volatile, a film that regularly defies expectations, and it had an inspired, yet thoughtful script. Said director Ron Howard: 'There's great conflict in the film and that makes for powerful, watchable drama.'

In other words, it's Gibson at his 'maverick' best, doing his own thing. The film culminates in a wild chase in and out of the New York traffic with Gibson jumping over taxis and helping to create mayhem in and around Madison Avenue. It seemed incredible that only a few weeks before, he had been hauled off an aircraft doubled up with pain and desperately in need of an emergency operation.

Said Gibson of his character Tom Mullin: 'He seems to have it all – money, loving family, great business – and then this happens to bring him back to what he is; a squirming mass of tingling nerves. He's horrified, terrified and he's made to suffer.'

The at times harrowing script, taken from a story by Cyril Hume and Richard Maibaum, was based on a 1956 film of the same title which starred Glenn Ford, Donna Reed and Leslie Nielsen, though director Ron Howard first heard of the earlier picture only a few weeks before shooting began on his own project. Howard was drawn to Ransom mainly because it was more edgy and tense than anything he had previously tackled. 'What was new to me as a film-maker, was the opportunity to examine, on an emotional level, the brutality and the intensity of contemporary life in a way that I never have,' he explained.

According to Howard, Gibson 'just seemed right for the part. I wanted the character to be a charismatic and believable contemporary hero, but on the other hand, he had to have an individualistic quality. To me, Mel has always seemed like a bit of a maverick.' Mel describes his character as a 'self-made guy, used to making hard decisions and taking gambles'. The fact that his character follows his instincts, against the official line and the well-intentioned advice of his friends and associates, held a strong appeal for Gibson. 'He believes he is right, but he can't be 100 per cent sure. It's torturous for him,' explained Mel.

It is a movie where the natural tensions are given extra depth and power by the clever technique of telling the story through the eyes and lifestyles, not just of the victims, but also of the criminals. Explains screenwriter Richard Price: 'I tried to set up two alternate families, the family of kidnappers and the family of the kidnapped. I was absorbed by the concept of giving weakness to the good people and strength to the bad people.' It is a modern morality tale.

Price's technique elicited a number of first-class portrayals from a largely experienced cast. Rene Russo had co-starred with Gibson four years before in *Lethal Weapon 3*. She was also, incidentally, a former high-school classmate of Ron Howard. Gary Sinise, the distinguished US stage actor, plays the fiercely convincing cop turned child-snatcher Jimmy Shaker. Other excellent portrayals are delivered by Delroy Lindo as the FBI agent Lonnie Hawkins, who handles the case from the Mullins' home, and Lili Taylor (Maris), Evan Handler (Miles) and Liev Schreiber (Clark) in the roles of the kidnappers. As Clark's brother and fellow villain, Howard cast Donnie Wahlberg, formerly of the pop group, *New Kids on the Block*. *Total Film* got it about right when they reported: 'Ransom offers strong characters, neat set-pieces, convincing central performances and an intriguing plot.'

More than one review, however, put *Ransom*'s main strength down to Gibson's own performance. 'The more sweaty and stroppy Gibson gets, the more gripping the film becomes,' claimed one. Another proclaimed: 'Mel Gibson is in excellent form in a thriller that shoots off in unexpected directions.' But the making of *Ransom* could have been a lot easier. That worst New York winter in twenty years slowed down the process of film-making at an important stage and the re-writing of sections of the script mid production was another hindrance. Shooting was running a month behind schedule at one point.

Gibson felt his character was too squeaky-clean in the earlier versions of the script. He needed to be flawed in some way. For all his success it was important, explained Gibson, that his character felt some guilt because he had earlier paid a bribe to a union leader to ward off a strike and was in urgent need of redemption. 'We needed to show his history, which included a situation where he didn't make the right decision and therefore he panics at the thought that he might be making the same mistake again,' Mel explained.

It was during the making of *Ransom* that Gibson fell ill on a private jet while flying from Los Angeles back to the film set in New York. The drama began at 33,000 feet over Montana, at first nothing much more than a niggling abdominal pain, but rapidly getting worse. Mel was given some medicine, which did nothing to ease his increasing discomfort. As the situation worsened, a call was put through for a car to be waiting at the airport and for a doctor to be on hand at his hotel.

'I thought it was food poisoning,' Gibson explained. 'But the pain got so much worse and I was shivering a lot that I knew it must be something else.' He said he did not feel he was going to die, but the pain was severe enough during the flight that he was worried about the absence of a doctor. When the limousine driver at the hotel failed to arrive, and Mel's condition was seriously worsening, a limousine booked for another guest was commandeered and he was rushed to hospital. At 3 a.m. surgeons removed a badly inflamed appendix. Within twenty-four hours he was out of bed and out of the hospital. Nevertheless, as Gibson was required for every scene, location shooting had to be postponed for two weeks.

Ransom, a Touchstone Pictures presentation, opened at number one at the North American box office and became one of the highest-grossing films of the year, taking more than $100 million towards the end of 1996, rapidly adding another $30 million. Its opening weekend in the United States netted $35 million, to make it the biggest Mel Gibson opening ever, even bigger than *Braveheart*, and the biggest ever for a non-cartoon Disney production. It was acclaimed in similar fashion when released in the UK in February 1997, occupying the top spot for several weeks.

Before *Ransom* was released Gibson was already busy shooting his next movie, *Conspiracy Theory*, a $13 million project. Here Gibson was reunited with his *Lethal Weapon* and *Maverick* director, Richard Donner. Once again Mel's fee was widely reckoned to be around the $20 million mark. So he made no complaints when reminded how tough life can be when picture commitments overlap. On one day's shoot he worked through until 5.30 the next morning on *Conspiracy Theory*, then kept a 9 a.m. meeting with the press to talk about *Ransom*. Jodie Foster was tipped to be his co-star in the new movie, but when she turned down the part Gibson and Donner approached Julia Roberts. Said producer Joel Silver: 'We needed not just an ingenue, but someone who could really pull their weight.'

The picture is about Jerry Fletcher (Gibson), an engaging, if paranoid New York cabbie, who reads weird implications into almost everything that life has to offer. For most of his fares Jerry's stories never move from first base, but then CIA psychiatrist Dr Jonas (Patrick Stewart) recognizes that one of his stories is 'uncomfortably close' to the truth. He details Justice Department attorney Alice Sutton (Julia Roberts) to keep tabs on Jerry.

The picture is marketed as an 'off-beat romantic thriller', but also contains some extremely chilling moments. The closer Fletcher gets to uncovering the CIA's secret the more violent Jonas becomes, but perhaps one of the fascinating aspects of *Conspiracy Theory* is that Gibson is cast more as a character actor than a typical leading man. 'But leading men are character actors,' responded Gibson, citing old-timers like Bogart and Cagney. 'Both were character actors and leading men,' he said. Because of the violence some concern was expressed about the picture's classification, though Donner and Silver were said to be confident since 'blood is not shown and Donner's deft directorial hand allows audiences' imagination to fill in what is not explicit'. The film was premiered in the United States on 25 July, 1997 – and with a satisfactory Certificate 15.

Celebrating his forty-first birthday in January that year Mel Gibson was generally more relaxed and reportedly looking fitter than he had done in years. When talking to journalists he seemed remarkably co-operative, modest, level-headed and contented. Acting was continuing to provide the adrenalin of life and he talked openly about his marriage, family and his faith in God. 'All my insecurities as a person are completely healed by acting,' he confided. He said that his wife Robyn had during black periods been his salvation on more than one occasion. 'I've told her many times that I need her and my children more than they need me,' he revealed.

Helping to sustain that seventeen-year marriage is his religious faith, believes Gibson. In 1996 he was the only Hollywood star to be invited to a special gathering of Catholic intellectuals and artists. In bringing up his large family, Gibson's philosophy is simple. He believes traditional values and discipline are important. He tells his children what is right and what is wrong and believes this in no way infringes on a child's freedom. 'Youngsters really do want some clear foundations laid down for them,' he has said. In the hedonistic world of Hollywood it is also rather refreshing that Gibson, for all his success, can still genuinely be embarrassed when an American poll taken shortly after *Braveheart* revealed that six out of ten women fantasize about him when they make love.

Gibson may not be the biggest-earning actor in Hollywood, though it is difficult to pinpoint someone who is consistently above him, but he is certainly there at the top of the list of power-players, a fact testified to by his on-going contract with Warner Brothers and contracts with Fox and Paramount. He is financially secure for life. Indeed, towards the end of the 1990s Mel Gibson had also carved himself a career as a successful businessman.

In April 1996 his company, Icon Productions, formed in 1989 after a rather messy break-up of Gibson's partnership with Patricia Lovell and now one of the busiest production companies in the United States, struck a three-year deal with Rupert Murdoch's Fox Film Entertainment to make movies in Sydney. The partnership became operational in 1997. This new film-making initiative was to operate from the Sydney Showground (renamed the Sydney Showground Studios), formerly home of the Sydney Agricultural Show. The New South Wales Government had sold the showground to Murdoch for the establishment of Australia's own film studios. The idea was for

Gibson and his business partner Bruce Davey to operate out of California while the Australian end would be looked after by film producer Timothy White. An early, tentative business plan looked at the prospect of five films to be made over a three-year period. The new deal, capable of revolutionizing the Australian film industry, made Gibson one of Hollywood's most powerful off-screen players and one of the most bankable people in the entertainment world today.

Yet Mel Gibson's rapport with the camera is as strong now as when he first charmed millions of picturegoers with the raw nakedness of that stunning gaze. In a poll conducted in mid 1997, 41 per cent of women voted Mel Gibson as the man they would most like to snuggle up to. And an enquiry held among American teenagers showed that they think Mel Gibson is the sexiest actor, with Bruce Willis (40 years old) at number two. Both left younger stars like Brad Pitt, Tom Cruise and Keanu Reeves far behind. But curiously enough, Mel Gibson is the supreme example of a Hollywood star who appeals strongly to both sexes.

Frances-M Blake, a committed and serious Gibson observer for some years, says:

> It has been reported, repeatedly, that he is the 'Sexiest Man Alive'. That theory does not have to be supported to explain his success. He is a very good-looking man and sexy of course, but he is also a funny, intelligent and talented actor. From *Tim*, all the way to *Ransom*, and *Conspiracy Theory* he is one of the most diverse of actors. He is also one of the shyest, self-effacing and modest men in the public eye.

Blake goes on:

> It is probably because there are contrary facets of personality, and the more a star, unusually, shies away from publicity, the more the public and the critics want to know and see about the person. Yet even with megastardom, he amazingly manages to come across as a really down-to-earth guy, with a healthy attitude towards child-rearing, home life and just getting on with it all.

But for his millions of fans, one dark cloud hovers just above the horizon. How long will Mel Gibson continue to be a star, up there on the silver screen? After all, the scale of his success has given him the luxury of working only on projects that appeal to him. His firmly established production company, together with his growing appetite for, and obvious abilities at, directing movies must both be taken as realistic pointers to the future. Even two years ago he caused minor panic when he said: 'People aren't going to want to see my ugly mush on the screen forever. Younger, better-looking people will come along.' Mind you, various so-called 'insider' sources have been predicting Gibson's Hollywood demise for years. One even said he would quit after *Hamlet*!

But surely, there is no immediate cause for concern. He is still a very big star indeed in Hollywood. Barry Norman has compared him with the great stars of the forties and fifties. Others have said that growing old suits him and is good for him, both in looks and as an actor. For the moment at least, Mel Gibson continues to get a buzz from appearing in front of the camera, even though the incentive to earn is not quite what it was years ago now he has an estimated fortune of . . . when confronted with the wealth question, a smiling Mel always trots out his standard answer: 'That's one of the great taboos, never talk money.'

In the United States, *Premiere* magazine in June 1997 placed Mel Gibson second only to, and just one point behind, Tom Cruise in their Global Star Power classification, an annual survey that ranks the worldwide bankability of stars. Reported the magazine: 'Star power is a little like real estate. If you're Tom Cruise or Mel Gibson, you own Hollywood. If you're Arnold Schwarzenegger or Harrison Ford or John Travolta or the other Tom (Hanks) or anyone on the A list, you've bought a hefty chunk. Everyone else is just renting.'

In any case, there is more solid evidence that the immediate future looks as bright as Gibson's immediate future has ever looked. As *Conspiracy Theory* was shooting its final scenes, Gibson was contemplating a retreat to his Malibu home for a few quiet weeks before considering his next move. There was already talk of him directing and possibly acting in a new adaptation of the Ray Bradbury novel *Fahrenheit 451*. Talk persisted about the satirical comedy which has incensed America's anti-smoking lobby, *Thank You For Smoking*, and there were rumours about a variety of other projects. A remake of the 1954 classic wartime legend of the *Dam Busters* seemed to be a strong contender, having captured Mel's imagination, with him in the role of his namesake, Guy Gibson VC. In addition, studio executives were said to be doggedly sweet-talking Gibson into reprising his *Mad Max* role, in return for a $25 million pay cheque – plus a percentage of the take, of course. More of a flyer, perhaps, was talk of a remake of *The Magnificent Seven*, though Mel has made no secret of his interest in doing another western some time.

Pushing through all this speculation was the sudden news that Mel had started location work in Chicago on a new picture called *Parker*, which quickly became *Payback*. To an extent based on the Lee Marvin 1967 thriller *Point Blank*, about a gangster who takes his revenge on a cheating partner, *Payback* was said to be more in tune with Richard Stark's novel *The Hunter*, which had been the baseline for both films.

Always lurking in the background of course, was *Lethal Weapon*. The series had by early 1997 notched up in excess of $700 million (£500 million) worldwide, and renewed pressure came from Warner Brothers after the huge success of *Ransom*. Could Mel be tempted? He had always stood out firmly against donning the mantle of Martin Riggs for a fourth time. But rumours of the biggest payout in film history might just help to change his mind. There had already been talk of a fee of $50 million (£30 million), with the assurance that Riggs would be killed off at the end.

Not a bad way to go, with Mel Gibson still there and ready to fight another day, should he wish – even as someone else.

Filmography

Summer City (Australia), 1978. Released through Interropic. Directed by Christopher Fraser. Produced by Phillip Avalon. Cast: John Jarrat, Phil Avalon, James Elliot, Steve Bisley, Mel Gibson, Debbie Foreman.

Mad Max (Australia), 1980. Released through American International. Directed by George Miller. Produced by Byron Kennedy. Appeared with Joanne Samuel, Hugh Keays-Byrne, Steve Bisley, Roger Ward.

Tim (Australia), 1980. Released through Satori Productions. Directed by Michael Pate. Produced by Michael Pate. Appeared with Piper Laurie, Alwyn Kurts, Pat Evison, Deborah Kennedy.

Attack Force Z (Australia), 1980. Released through United Artists. Directed by Tim Burstall. Produced by Les Robinson and John McCallum. Appeared with John Phillip Law, Chris Heywood, Sam Neill, John Waters.

Gallipoli (Australia), 1981. Released through Paramount Pictures. Directed by Peter Weir. Produced by Robert Stigwood and Patricia Lovell. Appeared with Mark Lee, Bill Kerr, Stan Green, Max Wearing.

Mad Max: The Road Warrior (US), 1982. Released through Warner Brothers. Directed by George Miller. Produced by Byron Kennedy. Appeared with Bruce Spence, Vernon Wells, Emil Minty, Mike Preston, Kjell Nilsson.

The Year of Living Dangerously (US), 1983. Released through MGM/US Entertainment Co. Directed by Peter Weir. Produced by James McElroy. Appeared with Sigourney Weaver, Linda Hunt, Michael Murphy, Noel Ferrier.

The Bounty (US), 1984. Released through Orion Picture Corporation. Directed by Roger Donaldson. Produced by Bernard Williams. Appeared with Anthony Hopkins, Laurence Olivier, Daniel Day-Lewis, Edward Fox, Bernard Hill, Tevaite Vernette.

The River (US), 1984. Released through Universal Pictures. Directed by Mark Rydell. Produced by Edward Lewis and Robert Cortes. Appeared with Sissy Spacek, Scott Glenn, Shane Bailey, Becky Jo Lynch.

Mrs Soffel (US), 1984. Released through MGM/UA Entertainment. Directed by Gillian Armstrong. Produced by Edgar J. Scherick, Scott Rudin, David Hicksay. Appeared with Diane Keaton, Matthew Modine, Edward Herrman, Trini Alvarado, Jennie Dundas.

Mad Max Beyond Thunderdome (US), 1985. Released through Warner Brothers. Directed by George Miller, George Ogilvie. Produced by George Miller. Produced by Richard Donner, Joel Silver. Appeared with Tina Turner, Helen Buday, Frank Thring, Bruce Spence, Angelo Rossitto.

Lethal Weapon (US), 1987. Released through Warner Brothers. Directed by Richard Donner. Produced by Richard Donner, Joel Silver. Appeared with Danny Glover, Gary Busey, Mitchell Ryan.

Tequila Sunrise (US), 1988. Released through Warner Brothers. Directed by Robert Towne. Produced by Thom Mount. Appeared with Michelle Pfeiffer, Kurt Russell, Raul Julia.

Lethal Weapon 2 (US), 1989. Released through Warner Brothers. Directed by Richard Donner. Produced by Richard Donner, Joel Silver. Appeared with Danny Glover, Joe Pesci, Joss Ackland, Patsy Kensit.

Bird on a Wire (US), 1990. Released through Universal Pictures. Directed by John Badham. Produced by Rob Cohen. Appeared with Goldie Hawn, David Carradine, Joan Severance.

Air America (US), 1990. Released through Guild/Indieprod/ Carolco. Directed by Roger Spottiswoode. Produced by Daniel Melnick. Appeared with Robert Downey Jnr, Nancy Travis, Ken Jenkins, David Marshall Grant, Lane Smith, Art La Fleur.

Hamlet (US), 1991. Released through Warner Brothers. Directed by Franco Zeffirelli. Produced by Dyson Lovell. Appeared with Glenn Close, Alan Bates, Ian Holm, Paul Scofield, Helena Bonham-Carter.

Lethal Weapon 3 (US), 1992. Released through Warner Brothers. Directed by Richard Donner. Produced by Richard Donner and Joel Silver. Appeared with Danny Glover, Joe Pesci, Rene Russo.

Forever Young (US), 1992. Released through Warner Brothers. Directed by Steve Miner. Produced by Bruce Davey. Appeared with Elijah Wood, Isabel Glasser, George Wendt, Jamie Lee Curtis.

The Man without a Face (US), 1993. Released through Warner Brothers. Directed by Mel Gibson. Produced by Bruce Davey. Appeared with Nick Stahl, Margaret Whitton, Fay Masterson, Gaby Hoffman.

Maverick (US), 1994. Released through Warner Brothers. Directed by Richard Donner. Produced by Bruce Davey and Richard Donner. Appeared with Jodie Foster, James Garner, Graham Greene, James Coburn, Alfred Molina.

Braveheart (US), 1995. Released through Twentieth Century Fox. Directed by Mel Gibson. Produced by Mel Gibson, Alan Ladd Jr., Bruce Davey. Appeared with Sophie Marceau, Patrick McGoohan, Catherine McCormack, Brenda Gleeson, James Cosmo, David O'Hara, Alun Armstrong, Angus McFadyen.

Ransom (US) 1997. Released through Touchstone Pictures.

Directed by Ron Howard. Produced by Scott Rudin, Brian Grazer, B. Kipling Hagopian. Appeared with Rene Russo, Brawley Nolte, Gary Sinise, Delroy Lindo, Lili Taylor, Liev Schreiber, Donnie Wahlberg.

Conspiracy Theory (US), 1997. Released through Warner Brothers. Directed by Richard Donner. Produced by Joel Silver and Richard Donner. Appeared with Julia Roberts, Patrick Stewart, Cylk Cozart, Stephen Kahan, Terry Alexander.

Index

203